GOODBYE

CONSTITUTION,

FREEDOM,

AMERICA

SMEA PUBLISHING

Cover picture credits go to: noisyroom.net/blog/2013/12/30/forum-what-are-your-predictions

Don Jans

ISBN

978-0-692-26976-3

Copyright – pending
2014

First Edition

SMEA publishing

FORWARD

I recognize much about who we are as Americans today, the state of our society, the direction in which we are headed from reading Don Jans fictional account of America as having become an informal Marxist state. Jans main character in this cautionary tale is out of step with the collectivist, amoral and grey atmosphere in which he lives and this book is about his main character's unlikely journey in terms of discovering truths. His main character gradually wakes up to certain realities due to a process that begins with his isolation from the mainstream as a young man and then evolves, through his experiences at College and at work, as he undergoes a process that leads him down a path of self-discovery and of no turning back.

In the course of the book Jans carefully describes Marxist philosophy and its practical effects by contrasting those ideas, in the form of clear point-by-point prose, with notions of American freedom. This exposition by the author raises in the mind of the reader an immediate reaction, sort of an "ah ha" moment, regarding how many freedoms been already stripped away by an authoritarian minded and intolerant left-wing culture and how these freedoms have disappeared without our even noticing that they are gone, right from under our noses.

The main character grows up and comes of age in a Marxist America, an amoral society that judges all equally and is thus devoid of human warmth and spirit, one in which people and families appear to be going through the motions like automatons who are unconscious of their condition. The society he describes seems almost dead and certainly bloodless. Nothing seems askew, however, and everything seems like it is in place.

The Author does not paint a situation at all like the outright Communist experiments of the past where the Bolsheviks in Russia or the Chinese Communists conducted open programs of mass murder and openly totalitarian seizure of all property. The type of Communism that he describes has been implemented so slowly and imperceptibly that it is almost not noticed. And those who occasionally do notice what is going on have a nasty habit of dying in accidents or committing "suicide."

The main character seems to be almost sleep-walking through the book even though he finds himself, almost in spite of himself; opposing the regime and finding threads of morality that make him vaguely aware of his own humanity. He operates in an atmosphere in which other human beings are virtually unaware of who they are as such concepts as an objective morality that exists out of reach of manipulation by the government and any form of an objective understanding of human nature had long ago been replaced by the alleged virtues of collectivism and the concomitant, albeit unconscious, surrender of individual freedom.

This book reminds me of comments made by Aldous Huxley, author of A Brave New World, during a speech at U. Cal - Berkeley shortly before his televised suicide. Huxley said:

There will be, in the next generation or so, a pharmacological method of making people love their servitude, and producing dictatorship without tears, so to speak, producing a kind of painless concentration camp for entire societies, so that people will in fact have their liberties taken away from them, but will rather enjoy it, because they will be distracted from any desire to rebel by propaganda or brainwashing, or brainwashing enhanced by pharmacological methods. And this seems to be the final revolution.

Don Jans, who has been touring the country and who is a regular guest on radio talk shows, is doing a great job of sounding the alarm in the face of the growing threat that seeks to gradually colonize our minds and souls. This book is an important and worthy part of his valiant efforts.

Written by: Chuck Morse, host of radio talk show "Chuck Morse Speaks", syndicated on the IRN/USA Radio Network, and author.

ACKNOWLEDGMENTS

Writing this book was very enjoyable. When I wrote my first book, "My Grandchildren's America," it was more of a struggle. This time, I had a better idea of how to proceed plus I chose to write a novel. I still have many people to thank. My son Eric kept encouraging me to write again, and he suggested I try a novel. My daughter Sara was supportive and along with Debbie, were the readers to give me my initial feedback. I also want to thank you Jake, for your creativity and your patience with me.

I do not envy anybody who does proof reading for me. Denise did a fantastic job correcting the initial draft and then Lynette and Emily came along to help with the final corrections and final feedback to help pull everything together so we could do the final work of preparing everything for the printer. Sara, this is always a challenge. You are becoming a real pro. You led the way and we got through it and the final product is now done.

Thank all of you so much. Words cannot express my gratitude.

PREFACE

Eric told me I should write a novel. That was about a year before I started my outline and writing. While I was traveling to speaking engagements, with time to think, this idea kept going through my mind. I finally settled on the idea and then started the process of doing the initial outline, the refining, and then the actual writing. The actual writing proved to be fun and very enjoyable.

I had my characters developed and knew the journey they would take. I must emphasize that any similarities between any characters mentioned in the book and any actual living or deceased person is strictly a coincidence. The one exception to this would be any reference to Karl Marx and Friedrich Engels. All other characters are fictitious, although the philosophies, concepts, and thoughts expressed by the characters are based in reality.

The evil the main characters oppose, and the situations they encounter are not fantasy. There are factions in our country that despise the capitalistic system and the freedoms we in this country enjoy. These factions do not express their true intent of fundamentally transforming the United States. They camouflage their real intent. This has always existed, but not as blatant as it is today

The situations the main characters oppose are happening this very day. The story line will keep you intrigued as you live through the trials and triumphs of these people. You will be able to relate to this reality just like the characters. You will recognize yourself in some of the situations although you may or may not understand from where the idea developed. Perhaps you will join the characters in their discussions. Mostly, you will come away with a much clearer understanding of the evil these people opposed and the evil that is in full force in the United States with the stated goal of fundamentally transforming the United States.

CONTENTS

Chapter 1.   Pg 12

Chapter 2.   Pg 27

Chapter 3.   Pg 45

Chapter 4.   Pg 67

Chapter 5.   Pg 94

Chapter 6.   Pg 116

Chapter 7.   Pg 134

Chapter 8.   Pg 151

Chapter 9.   Pg 171

CHAPTER 1

It was a cold January morning. The wind was blowing the light snow that had fallen the previous evening across the road, as the car sped toward the small town 25 miles away. The outside thermometer said, it was minus ten degrees. It wasn't much warmer in the old blue Chevy. He was anxious to get to that small town where the nearest hospital was located. His wife was in labor and was about to have their third child. They were hoping this one would be a girl since their two older children were boys. They had already bought a pink baby blanket, thinking that would insure that this baby would be the daughter they so desperately wanted.

Five days later he was driving down that very same road. This time he and his wife were headed toward the small town where they lived. It was much warmer than it had been when they were in a rush to get to the hospital. The sun was shining brightly and there was no wind. It even felt warm in the old blue Chevy. His wife had the new baby wrapped in the pink baby blanket and had placed the baby in the back seat in a tiny bassinet. They were not singing as they did when they had made this same trip when their first two baby boys were born. Those were joyful trips. They were just happy the boys were healthy. This baby was also healthy. This baby was also a boy. Both he and his wife felt resentment. They had planned to have only three children, but they both really wanted a girl in the family. This third child just did not fit into their plans. They both agreed they would not replace the pink baby blanket with a blue one. After all, this child had totally disrupted their life plans, and they were not about to make any special accommodation for him, now or in the future.

Both knew they would have to clothe and feed the child, and even act like they were happy. That is what you did in these small towns in the heartland of America. It was very important to them what others in the town thought. Everybody knew everybody else and most of them knew the business of their neighbors. Much of their extended family lived in the same town or very near. Once in a while one of the nieces, nephews, or cousins would venture outside the county boundaries and, even rarer, was when one ventured out of the state. They had no choice but to act happy. But within their home, the resentment toward the child could not be hidden from him or his brothers.

As this child grew, he always believed he was different. Physically he was always a smaller child. He had to start wearing very thick glasses before he was two years old. He loved to be outside playing with his older brothers. Being a two year- old he would lose his glasses or put the glasses in places for safekeeping, but then forget where the safe keeping place was. The parents were not wealthy people. When the glasses had to be replaced, it was a financial burden on the family. The father was not a patient person. The little boy would be physically punished and verbally humiliated every time the glasses search took place, which was often.

As the child grew he became somewhat of a loner. He learned if he stayed to himself he would not hear the verbal abuse from his parents or his brothers. He was unable to defend himself against the constant physical attacks of his brothers. His mind was quicker than his brothers. He learned he was able to out spar them verbally, which, was not in his best interest, physically. His brothers justified their physical abuse because of the boy's smart mouth. The parents could not verbally spar with the boy either. Even while he was a young boy, the parents would side with the older brothers and only tell them they should be more careful not to hurt their little brother.

Finally the day came when he would start first grade at the local school. All grades, including the high school students, had classes in the same building. He adapted to school life; in fact, thrived in school. Learning was never difficult and he was one of the rare boys who enjoyed learning. He read books, not because they were an assignment, but because he wanted to read the book. History was his favorite subject. His recreational reading, which was constant, would most often be a biography of an American hero. Over time, this expanded to include historical figures from all of history. He also expanded his reading from primarily biographies to different historical events and time periods.

His search for knowledge and learning wasn't restricted to history. He was always interested in why people did what they did. He would wonder why people were so predictable. When he would talk to his friends, he would ask why they did what they did. Mostly, the answers would be based on others' expectations- their parents, their other friends, their siblings, their teachers, or others in the community. This mystified him. He never did remember positive reinforcement from those who would normally give it to children- their parents and siblings- since it was impossible for him to please his parents or siblings and receive positive feedback he learned not to be concerned with their expectations. This taught him at a very young age, even before he could reason; he should not to be concerned with what others think to determine his course of action. He learned at a very young age to think and to act, based on his own judgment. This was the most valuable lesson his parents, or anyone, could have taught him.

It proved, however, to cause problems for him at home, at school, and in many social situations. He was a pleasant child, and, for the most part, well behaved. He would not go out of his way to cause problems or be disruptive. He was trustworthy and a hard worker. He had started to mow lawns for people by the time he was seven. The going rate was fifty cents an hour. Adults would be quick to ask him if he would do odd jobs for them because he would be the first one on the job, and not take breaks until the work was done. Farmers around the area would always include him in groups of boys they would hire to clean their fields of rocks. This was called rock picking. It was dirty, hot, and hard work. It paid fifty cents an hour. When he was older, he would be included in the groups who were hired to help the farmers with their harvesting. He never complained about the job he was given, even when he was the person who shoveled the grain as it was dumped into the enclosed building. This was the dirtiest of all jobs. The dust from the grain had no place to escape, so it just hung in the air, and breathing for anybody inside the building was very difficult. The dust also caused the skin to itch. The best thing about this job was it taught a person to really appreciate fresh air and showers.

He caused problems for himself because he would always ask why. When his parents would explain that something was to be done a certain way, he wanted to know why it had to be done in that fashion. If he were told it was because that was how it was always done or what other people expected, he would want to know why that was important. He wanted to know why we should be concerned with what other people might think. He wanted to know why that was important, since it did not make much sense to him. "Because" was not a good enough answer for him either. He would then explain how he thought it should be done and why. Kids were not to contradict their parents, he was reminded many times. This was not important to him, since he had stopped seeking the approval of his parents before he was old enough to understand that was what he was doing.

This questioning attitude caused problems for him in school, as well. The school administrators and the teachers were not used to students asking them why, and then expecting an explanation. Most of the administrators and teachers resented having to explain, especially to a child. Most of the time, the administrators and teachers had no explanation, because they had never wondered why. The administrators and teachers did what they were told to do. The administrators and teachers did what others expected of them. The administrators and teachers were concerned with what others thought. This was a problem, not only with teachers, but also with coaches. Periodically a teacher or coach would appreciate this inquisitive mind. Periodically a teacher would appreciate a very good student who was concerned with not only how, but also what, and why.

Socially, he was known as a kid with an attitude. Many adults thought of him as just a smart-mouthed kid who had no right to question them; after all, they were the adults and he was the kid. The adults certainly did not owe this kid an explanation. After all, this is how it had always been done and so this is how it should be done now. "Because" had always been a good enough answer and it should be good enough for this kid. His attitude also caused a problem for him on the playground. The older kids were not sure how to respond to him. They had no idea why things were done a certain way. They had never asked "why". If they could just accept things as they had always been done, why couldn't he? Who does he think he is?

His work ethic, coupled with his quick mind, taught him if he wanted new things, he would have to provide them for himself. This valuable lesson would bode well for him in the years to come. When you were the third boy in a family that looked to stretch every dollar, your new clothes for the school year were the hand- me-downs from the older brothers. This was also true for baseball gloves, bikes, ice skates, and all the other things boys in that little town in the American heartland wanted. His first prized possession he remembered buying with his own money was a Spaulding baseball glove. He knew it had to be a very good glove because this was one of the brands the Major Leaguers used.

His love of history became a love of politics as well. While most of the boys in that little town would read only the sports page of the newspaper, he would read the political news, first, and then the sports page news. He understood there were two political parties. He would hear political discussions taking place about town, especially around election time. The men especially, would become emotional when discussing the subject. They would speak in vague and general terms, declaring one candidate was a "commie," and the men with whom they were arguing, would shout back that the other guy was just a "war monger." The kids on the school playground would also argue, always using the same clichés their parents used. He would ask these people what it meant to be a "commie;" what does it mean to be a "war monger;" why should the government collect more taxes; what does it mean to be free; why should the farmer be paid when he does not even plant his crops? There were so many questions he had, but he could not get answers from these people, that made sense.

As he grew older, he started to understand much more clearly the biographies and history he had read. He began to understand there were different philosophies. He understood there were people who believed the institution that was called government, was intrusive, and that less government was better government. Others had the opposite view. These people believed the government was there to take care of people and to control business and society. He had learned from his early childhood, that when people gave you something, they expected something in return. He had to become very independent at a very young age, and did not believe he was indebted to, or dependent upon anybody. Because of his development years, he believed less government was better, but did not totally understand why. Listening to the adults around election time did not clarify anything, since he learned they did not understand, either.

Even though few people in this small town ever went on to college - none from his family had ever gone on to college - he never talked about if he would go to college, but where. He always knew he would go to the University. He had begun saving at a very young age and knew he would have to work while at school, but that was just what had to be done.

While he was at University, he began to get answers to some of his why questions. His question about the government and the role it should play became much clearer, along with many other questions he had, when he read a book that had been written by a Senator. The Senator outlined in this book what a conservative is, what he believes, and why. What a great eye opener that book was for him.

The book explained that there are two basic ideologies. One side believes in the goodness of government, and that the role of government is to take care of the citizens. This side, often referred to as the left, liberal, or progressives, believes government exists to do all things. The other side is commonly referred to as the right, or conservatives. The conservative side believes limited government is the best government. The conservative adheres to the principles of the constitution, which has as one of those principles, to limit government. The reason the conservative believes in limited government, the Senator said, was because throughout history government has proved to be the chief instrument for thwarting man's liberty. Government represents power, in the hands of a few men, to control and regulate the lives of other men. Power corrupts men; and thus the axiom "absolute power corrupts absolutely." The less power the government has, the more power and thus freedom the people have.

The Senator went on to explain that the conservative believes government does not have an unlimited claim on the earnings and other personal property of the citizen. Unlike the liberal or progressive, who believes all income and personal property belongs to the government, and it is the government who decides how much of those earnings and personal property they will allow the citizen to retain.

He also read in this clearly - written book by the Senator that the conservative believes in the individuality, independence, ingenuity, and self-reliance of the individual. Differences between individuals strengthen the whole society, the book explained. This is why the conservative believes in freedom of choice. But along with this freedom, the individual is also responsible for the consequences of those choices; that is, success or failure. The liberal or progressive believes that individuals should be limited in their choices, because they believe the government is more capable of making better choices for the individual. The liberal or progressive, the Senator explained, believes all citizens should adhere to the dictates of the government and conforms to the desires and decisions of the collective. The liberal or progressive also advocates that the individual, as a part of the collective, is, therefore, not responsible for the consequences of his decisions, since the decisions were not the responsibility of the individual. Because of this, the individual will share fairly in the proceeds of the success of the collective as a whole. The rewards will be limited and the consequences of the failures will be limited. Society will be conforming, and social status and economic status will be equal for all, so believe the liberals and progressives.

Now that he understood the essence of the beliefs and values of the conservative versus liberals, or progressives, as these beliefs and values related to the role of government in society, he realized he had been a conservative for as long as he could remember. It was, or at least had become his nature, to believe society is much stronger when comprised of strong, independent, and self-reliant individuals who wanted to be responsible for the consequences of their decisions; successes or failures. He had always understood a homogenous and conforming society, as the liberals or progressives advocated through a controlling government with belief in the collective, was destructive to growth and advancement for all. He had seen in his own life that when he had failed and had to take responsibility for those failures, it made him stronger, more resourceful, and more innovative. He realized how refusing to just accept answers and not ask why, hindered and restricted the growth of the individual and the society. He also became very thankful for his upbringing. He was beginning to understand that the situation and circumstances of his childhood were greatly responsible for whom he had become and was becoming.

Having come to the realization of whom he was, and perhaps why he had become a conservative, brought him peace of mind. It did not, however, make his time at the University any easier, nor did it subdue his quest to understand why. He found the desire to understand why would expand to an even greater hunger. This hunger would lead him to want to know if, what was being taught as truth was, in fact, truth, and the reality of history. He had learned as a toddler, and through life up to now, that it is critical to always verify, with thorough research, that what is being portrayed as history and reality, is really what had happened. He learned in academia, where he had been taught the search for truth and expansion of ideas was paramount, the idea to verify with thorough research, was frowned upon by many professors, and loathed by others.

CHAPTER 2

The excitement of being at the University, away from the scorn and disparaging comments was what he had dreamed of for years. Here, he believed everybody would want to know why. Here he believed everybody would welcome, yes, even encourage you, to question all conclusions in that elusive quest for truth. He already understood more about who he was in his first couple of months at University, than he had in all the time prior to matriculating.

As exciting as that discovery was, the first two years proved to be unexciting and uneventful so far as his academic studies were concerned. He had to take classes that were of little interest to him. Like so many first and second - year students, he took classes that were mandatory so he would have, what was called, a well-rounded education. He would go to class and sit in huge auditoriums, listening to uninspiring teachers' assistants droning on and on. He quickly learned, however, it was important to do well in these classes, so he exercised a newly acquired skill he called mind control, or convincing yourself, that the course you were forced to take to satisfy the requirements, was the most important subject to you for that time period. Since that time period was only three months, it was possible to do, and it proved to be successful for him.

These first two years were important for other reasons as well. He learned that being at University was also very educational outside the classroom. Yes, there was a social aspect to school, as well. The temptations to forget about the reasons he had dreamed about being there were great. Constantly he was being bombarded with offers to attend this social gathering or that one. These were not limited to Friday and Saturday nights; but every night of the week seemed to have some special reason why you should be at a social gathering. The temptation wasn't that Wednesday happened to be hump day that made the gathering so difficult to resist, but charming and interesting co-eds would also be in attendance. These co-eds even seemed to be interested in mind - expanding topics. He would later learn that some of them really were.

With all of these distractions, he quickly learned that discipline would need to be developed if he was to remain at the University. Part of this discipline was to set priorities that included setting specific times to concentrate on academics so he had time to also enjoy the very interesting and intriguing attributes of the co-eds. What helped him in setting these priorities were the limitations on his time.   In his first week at University, he had to find work so he could continue his education. After all, tuition, books, fees, room and board, and entertainment were his responsibility. His father had promised that he would be given financial help, but it never came. Budgeting was always a challenge. It was always a pleasant surprise when he would find he had a couple extra dollars in his pocket on a Friday night when he was done with work.

By the end of his first quarter he had been able to develop a nice routine that worked for the rest of his time at University. He would spend time between classes in the library so as not to get caught in a game of cards, or a fun, but meaningless, conversation with the guys. Evenings, during the week, were for work. Friday evening, after work and Saturday evening were for social gatherings and corresponding periphery activities. Athletic events were special and worked great for dating, especially since the activity fee all students paid, included the athletic events.

He did not perfect his skills to manage his time or his priorities, but it would be safe to say he had developed them and he was getting better and better all the time at managing them. Why time management was so critical became evident at the end of the second quarter of his first year at school. His friends, who had mastered the art of the social gatherings every evening, including many of the charming and wonderful co-eds, were not around for spring quarter in his first year of school. If they had only known that spring quarter was the best, maybe they would have learned that critical rule of life; our choices do have consequences.

It was at the beginning of the third year of school, when the classes were smaller and were taught by the professors and not the teachers' assistants that he begin to have classroom intrigue. The professors did not like the question why, just like his parents, teachers, older schoolyard kids, and other adults he knew as a child. These professors not only did not like the question why, they did not like to be asked to explain why they drew certain conclusions. Even though he had learned to an acceptable degree the art of managing time and choices, he never did learn the art of accepting what he was told was truth without wanting to explore the facts and determine for him, if it indeed, was truth. He had learned by this time the difference between opinion and fact or subjectivity and objectivity. Not accepting that the opinions or subjective thoughts of the people in authority who made the statements, made them fact, caused him difficult times and a substantial amount of extra work. The extra work did turn out to be a blessing and not a curse.

In his first two years, his classes in history were more fact based. He was taught the timing of events and how, for instance, the French Revolution had an effect on the happenings in countries as far away as Russia. When Catherine learned of the overthrow and then the killing of the Bourbons, she feared that could also happen in Russia and she became more cautious and took more precautions regarding her position as Czarina. The Hapsburgs became very aware, as well, especially since the Queen of France, who was a victim of the Revolution, was a Hapsburg daughter. These types of happenings he found to be very interesting, and it certainly helped him gain a better perspective on how the events in one part of the world have an impact on events and people in other parts of the world.

Even the history of the United States was more fact based with fewer reasons to ask why. For the most part, the discussions of the various players seemed to be more objective than subjective. Of course the role of Benjamin Franklin was always interesting to discuss. Was he a true rebel and patriot or was he just an opportunist who switched sides when he believed it to be in his best interest? Was he a wise diplomat or simply a charming, whimsical man who had an eye for the ladies, a taste for liquor, and was an opportunist who knew he could allow people like John Adams and Thomas Jefferson do the real negotiating, and then he would take the credit? Whatever Franklin was, did not really matter since he was not a player with a role that ever made much of a difference, like a Washington, Adams, Jefferson, Madison, or Hamilton and on and on. Never the less, he was interesting and he was around.

When the study of the United States came to the time of the great depression and World War II, he learned what the rewriting of history really meant. Even in high school, he had done a substantial amount of reading and studying about the times of Franklin Roosevelt. He found that much of what he was taught in his first two years at University was not what he had read and learned, not in high school, but on his own. This revision of history became very pronounced in his classes in his last two years at University with professors' opinions and conclusions not corresponding to his reading and understanding. He also found a dramatic difference between professors' opinions and conclusions in their analysis of the role of individualism vs. collectivism and private ownership of productive property vs. community ownership of productive property.

Although his understanding of these two areas being so different from what the professors were teaching would cause him much extra work during his time at University, it proved critical for him in later years. Even after he had learned the consequences, he still would not answer a question the way the professor expected him to answer just to please the professor and insure a good grade. He learned to articulate clearly and succinctly his thoughts and ideas, always backing them with the appropriate supporting information. In order to do this, he had to learn to do his research, which helped him understand even more clearly the differences and the long-term effect or results of these happenings. This clear understanding would help him in his early business years and cause him great problems in his later years.

These professors were claiming Franklin Roosevelt was a great President and his economic policies were responsible for bringing the United States out of the Great Depression. They also were teaching Franklin Roosevelt was a Great War leader and was one of the best if not the greatest President.

He became the target of one professor, when the professor explained how FDR, through his New Deal policies, had brought the United States out of the Depression. Not being able to resist, he asked the professor if the professor would explain why the unemployment rate in 1938 was just below 20%, about the same as when Roosevelt was inaugurated the first time in 1933. The professor explained how the unemployment rate had dipped to 15% in 1937. He was on a roll and had to ask if the professor could then explain why the United States went into another deep recession in late 1937 and 1938. During this exchange, what was most surprising to him was not that the professor still proclaimed the policies of the New Deal, but that the other students seemed stunned and surprised by his documented numbers.

Later, in that same class, after the professor explained how important the Blue Eagle Program under the National Industrial Recovery Act was, he could see by the look on the faces of the other students they had no idea what this program was. He could not resist again, and asked the professor to explain how the program helped the small business when it prevented them from selling goods or performing services below the price of the large manufacturer and service provider. After the professor tried to explain this program was good for all, he had to ask, then why was Fred Perkins in York, Pennsylvania jailed for selling batteries at a reduced price, why was Jacob Maged of Jersey City, New Jersey jailed for pressing pants at $.35 as opposed to $.40 and why were Sam and Rose Markowitz of Cleveland, Ohio jailed for cleaning suits at $.05 under the mandated $.40 rate, jailed? He probably should have stopped at that point but when you are on a roll, you are on a roll. So he continued and asked why the Supreme Court, not only ruled the Blue Eagle Program as unconstitutional, but broke into laughter when they learned the law had gone so far as to require the Schechter brothers of Brooklyn to require that their customers could not choose the chickens they wanted to buy. Under the code, it was explained, "The customer is not permitted to select the chickens he wants. He must put his hand in the coop when he buys and take the first chicken that comes to hand." The professor did not answer because of the laughter of the other students. The professor immediately dismissed class, but told him to remain. The professor then explained he would fail the class if he opened his mouth in class, again.

Despite the ultimatum by the professor, two good things came from the exchange. As he was leaving the classroom, several of the students were waiting for him to express their gratitude and their delight at exposing the foolishness of the bureaucrats. Included in this group was a delightful co-ed who lingered behind the others to walk with him. This led to sharing a soft drink, which led to a delightful relationship over the next several months. He also learned, that despite this pleasant outcome, he should always ask questions in these classroom settings with the intent of learning from the professor, regardless of the professors' prejudices.

In future classes dealing with the FDR time period, he was able to ask questions in different classes with different professors, and did gain some understanding of how the apologists thought. Questions he asked included: How did government rationalize the methods of the NRA in dealing with the public, and how did they believe that by requiring a business to charge the public more, it would benefit the economy; how did the destruction of food - grains and animals - benefit the economy and relieve the hunger so rampant in the country; how did the dramatic increase in excise and income taxes help the economy in such dire financial times; were not FDR's policies what caused the elongation of the depression and actually brought about the recession in late 1937 and 1938? The answers given by the different professors were defensive, protecting their theory that FDR was a great President. The reason they believed and taught this was always based on ideology and not actual results.

As he moved on to world politics and world history in his fourth year at University, he found this same type of reasoning by the professors would be predominate when discussing the collective approach to society as put forth by

Karl Marx. That reasoning meant the professors would answer his questions based on their belief in the ideology put forth by Marx, and not the historical results this philosophy produced. He would come to understand the reasoning of these ideologues, although never agreeing with their conclusions. He also found there were fewer students in the classes, but the number of students that agreed with the professors' philosophy and conclusions, was nearly unanimous.

In the different classes he would ask different questions based on concepts he knew Karl Marx had taught in his different writings. When talking about individual ownership of productive property such as farmland; he asked why it was wrong for the individual farmer to own the property, and be responsible for the production on his land, as opposed to the state owning the land and the farmer producing for the state. He explained when Lenin mandated this latter policy in the early days of the Bolshevik takeover, the production decreased dramatically. When Lenin allowed partial private ownership, production increased dramatically. The professor gave the standard answer that much of the result was due to weather, and the

Bolsheviks had not yet learned to run the collective farms efficiently.

In another class he asked the professor what Karl Marx really meant when he wrote "from each according to his abilities to each according to his needs." It was explained by the professor that this is the most efficient and fair means by which society can operate. The professor said having all the needs of people met, was the most freeing of all economic concepts. If the individual knows his basic needs were covered, he could do the type of work that satisfies him, individually. It gave the individual the freedom to do different things without concerning himself about the proficiency or productivity of his work. When one of the other students innocently asked why would the productive worker produce to his maximum ability if he did not receive rewards for his effort, the professor used the tired rationale that in this perfect society, when the factors of accumulation and greed had been negated through egalitarianism, all would put forth their maximum effort because this is how the individual would be fulfilled. He wanted to ask why that result had never happened in any society where this concept had been tried, but refrained from asking because he knew he would be sarcastic.

In another class, when the discussion turned to the expansions and contractions of economic cycles, the professor explained these recessions, and even devastating depressions, were caused by the greed, mismanagement, and inefficiencies inherent in capitalism. The professor went on to say that a system that eliminates the motive of greed would always have an economy that will expand at an even pace, consistent with the growth of the population. The question was asked by a student if this was desirable, or would it be more desirable to grow at a consistent rate greater than the growth of population; would this not constantly raise the standard of living in society. He thought, what a great question, but already knew the answer the professor would give. Right on cue, the professor explained that when you grow at a rate greater than the population, excess is created. It is this excess that unleashes the evil of greed, and within a short time the equilibrium and egalitarianism would have been replaced by a greedy capitalistic society and all the evils of capitalism will again appear. The equilibrium and egalitarianism are of greater benefit to society than the evil that an increase in the standard of living would affect, the professor explained. He had raised his hand, but the bell rang just at that moment, and perhaps saved him from himself, for he was about to ask the professor why, and could you please cite examples.

In another class dealing with religion and philosophy, the discussion included the teaching of Karl Marx. The professor was explaining how the practice of Marxism would bring about a very stable society that would eliminate all the evils associated with ambition. Since all would be equal politically, socially, and economically, nobody would be concerned or even tempted to distort, cheat, and manipulate others to get ahead. Getting ahead would lose all meaning, since what a person had would be based solely on need. He jumped into this discussion and asked if this was the reason Marx said there was no need for long standing principles, morality, or religion. The professor stated, to his surprise, that was a wonderful and enlightened observation. The professor amplified by explaining that when capitalism, with its evil of greed, is erased; there will be no reason for principles, religion, or morality. The concepts of religion and morality, the professor explained, have just served to restrict the acceptance of all people for who they are, and have been a hindrance to society by generating prejudices. Another student asked if mankind can exist without the restrictions principles, religion, and morality place on harmful behavior. The professor explained that was absurd, for when the element of greed is eliminated and all people are equal, there is no need for the damaging restrictions and beliefs of religion or morality. The freedom for people to be who they are and the acceptance of such, will be totally freeing to all society.

In his last quarter at University, he was taking a class on different forms of government and how Marxism related to governments. The professor was explaining how Marxism is ever evolving; it, Marxism, is not an end, but a process. The process brings society to a more free state at every stage of development. Becoming intrigued by the spirit of the discussion, he asked two questions: Why then did Marx say the freedom, independence, and individuality of the capitalist had to be abolished; would not this theory of freedom say these should become greater? He went on and questioned when would the totalitarian state or despotic conditions called for by Marx be abolished, and the days of absolute freedom begin? The first of the questions was simply dismissed by the professor, explaining the question had no relevance, since the evil capitalist would have been abolished, one way or the other. So far as the totalitarian state and despotism were concerned, the professor said in all states where total freedom was the end result, the beginning stages had to be orchestrated, by at times, unpleasant actions. This was the price that had to be paid to eliminate all the evil capitalism had produced and would linger without despotic means to totally eliminate them. He asked if the professor could cite any examples where any freedom, much less absolute freedom, was the end result of totalitarian government. This time the professor was saved by the bell.

He also had discussions with different students in informal educational settings and totally social settings. What he learned from these discussions was that many students believed in the concept of collectivism or Marxism, as opposed to individualism or capitalism. When he would ask them the differences, the answers were predictable and wrote: collectivism is about people and capitalism is about greed, with collectivism being compassionate and good, and individualism being selfish and bad. When he would ask for examples, the standard answer was that the ideal had not yet been achieved, but it was evolving and, in time, it would prevail. He could only conclude these ideas were products of indoctrination and not education, understanding that indoctrination is when the student is given the answer and charged with proving it, and education is when the student is given the problem and asked to study and arrive at his own conclusion, outlining his research and reasoning.

He graduated on the early plan; that was, he graduated one quarter early. It was interesting how many of his acquaintances and friends who advocated collectivism was on the five, six, and even seven-year plans. His time at the University had truly been educational. He had asked the question why many times and about many things. What he had learned would benefit him greatly in later life. The two most important things he learned was to never stop asking why and he started to understand the thinking of the Marxist/Progressive with all their inconsistencies, irrationalities, misconceptions, and hypocritical ideas

CHAPTER 3

Having learned discipline and planning, he was able to graduate from the University at the end of winter quarter in his fourth year, ahead of the large group graduating in the spring. The economy was not even keeping pace with the growth of population. The unrest in the Middle East had brought a spike in the price of oil. With the ideological war being waged against the production of fossil fuels around the world, and especially in the United States, the price of gasoline, jet fuel, and diesel was at record highs and setting new record highs almost monthly. The occupant of the White House had told the American people they must lower their expectations. To people like him, people who had studied the American Revolution, the United States Constitution, and the Federalist papers, this attitude was appalling. America was founded on fighting great odds and achieving the impossible. After all, how could this rag tag group of colonists defeat the strongest nation in the world at that time?

With this being the economic and political setting, the potential of finding a good paying job with real stability was unlikely. Fortunately for him, a government regulatory agency was hiring and he just happened to hear about it from one of the alumni at the fraternity house. Not having many other possibilities and not having the resources to try to start his own business, he decided he would call for an interview. This was one of the situations where timing in life was everything. The interview went very well. He did not realize this at the time, but he would later learn government interviews were not like private company interviews. The government was not concerned with ambition, innovation, or if you were a self-starter. They were far more interested in your background and your grades. His background was very good since he had come from a small town and his parents were middle class. The fact that he had graduated early and with a very acceptable grade point average made him a "lock."

The position sounded exciting to him. It required that he be able and willing to travel constantly. Some of the travel would be regional, but there would also be much national travel required. He had only been to four states in the country up to that time. He had dreamed of traveling beyond the plain states. How exciting it would be to go around the country, including cities of which he had only dreamed; cities like New York, Los Angeles, Washington DC, San Francisco, and yes even Chicago, St. Louis, and Dallas. The government would pay him a very nice income. They would also pay for his transportation and lodging expenses plus pay him a very generous per diem. It really sounded too good to be true. He got lost in the excitement, but remembered that the work he would be expected to do was to audit and verify that people in private industry were following the rules and regulations established by the government regulators to maintain the safety of the America publics' assets.

After he had completed the interview he was introduced to several people with titles that he did not remember. It seemed to him there were undersecretaries to undersecretaries of secretaries. He finally met the person that seemed to be responsible for making the final decision. This person was the head of Human Resources for that division. The head was a reserved person with a very limp handshake. This person made it clear it was his decision as to who was hired, and although he had a very good chance and met all the qualifications, the final decision could not be made for five business days. Those were the regulations and regulations could not be violated, so Human Resources would not contact anybody before five days. The Human Resources person then took more time than the actual interview had taken, explaining all the regulations that had to be followed, both before the final decision could be made and even more regulations that had to be followed after the decision was made, if positive. When he asked the Human Resource person his first why questions, he was told that you do not ask why when the regulation says this is how it is done. If the regulation states that this is how it is done, that is the way you do it.

This should have been a red flag, but with the excitement of seeing the country and being paid to do so, it was not a difficult decision for him to listen and not ask why. That strategy proved successful, because on the morning of the sixth day he received a call from Human Resources announcing to him that he was approved, and the government regulatory agency would like him to be a part of them. The timing was fantastic. He graduated from University on a Tuesday evening and reported for his first day of work for the government on the next Monday.

This was just enough time for him to get himself somewhat settled. He did not know where he would call home, as of yet, so it made no sense to get an apartment. That would come later. He needed to go through his clothes and discard many of his standbys. His remaining wardrobe would prove adequate for the training period and hopefully, for the first couple of weeks of work. He would have received a couple of paychecks by that time, and since the government was paying for his housing, and giving him per diem during this training period, he would be able to accumulate a little money and start adding to his wardrobe.

The two-week training school was a great indication of what was to follow. He learned the training class was a preview of the inefficiency, the arrogance, and the outright wastefulness of what the government had become. The very first day of training he was, as usual, early. A couple of the other trainees also arrived early, but most arrived right at the stated hour, except for the instructor. The instructor arrived 15 minutes late, only to explain that the class should take a break while he located the training materials. The class finally started an hour late. The rest of the morning class was the instructor complaining about the inefficiency and the wasted time that was a part of government work, so the class better get used to it. The afternoon training was the instructor explaining to the class that their new job was very important, because if it were not for them, those private greedy companies would take advantage of the public who were not smart enough to understand what was in their best interest.

And so the two weeks were to go with some actual training of what appeared to be arcane and/or punitive rulings and regulations. The training was centered on how the new agents would search for generally small insignificant violations. When they had discovered such a violation, it was to be reported to the chief of the crew, who would then use the violation to threaten the institution with a lawsuit brought by the government. The way for the institution to avoid the lawsuit was to pay a fine that was less than the cost of the lawsuit.

He did get to know the other trainees, both in class and in the evenings. He quickly learned he liked and respected very few of the other trainees. Most of the trainees were very excited about being able to trick those greedy and cruel business owners, as they called them, into returning some of their ill-gotten profits back to the government so the government could give them back to the exploited people.

Early in the training period he asked those trainees why they believed that profits were not earned, and in fact, evil. The answers were frightening to him. The answers were the talking points of the professors at the University who had explained that any profit really belongs to the worker and is not earned income to the owner since the owner did no work for it. He asked these trainees if they believed the investment and the risk the owner was taking so the worker had a job, was not worthy of the profit they received. He was told the investment was nothing more than money stolen from the worker, and the company should not be privately owned by the owners and investors, but the community or the people should own it. Therefore, they said, by finding ways to return that stolen profit to the people, they would be serving the community.

He thought he should look for a different position at least once every day of training. He was able to get through training knowing he had a paycheck in a very difficult economy. Plus, the allure of the travel, and seeing other parts of the country was too exciting to give up. He also rationalized, that when he actually was in the field, other agents would think like he did; that, in fact, he would truly audit to help the institution be a more efficient and financially strong company, which would protect and serve the public. After all, this is what he was told the position would be when he interviewed and also what he had read on the website.

He was one of the top trainees in the class. He was one of the few who were able to request a group to which they would be assigned. He chose to be assigned to the national traveling pool. The members of the traveling pool would go to different areas of the country to help when the regional groups were behind or to help when the regional group would be working in one of the larger institutions and needed additional personnel. Not only would he be able to travel, but also he would work with different people and be exposed to many different types of business situations. This proved to be very valuable to him when he left government work. The schedule proved to be quite difficult socially, since he was most often gone for two weeks at a time. He would then have a long weekend at home, getting home on a Thursday evening and leaving the next Monday morning. This gave him enough time to get laundry done, repack for the next two week trip, and have an evening or two free.

The whole experience was truly educational and eye opening. He was able to see the major cities in the United States and many of the secondary cities as well. In the next few years he would have been in every state in the union, including Hawaii and Alaska. When gone, he would spend several days in one city, so he was able to become familiar with the city. He would go to most of the cities several times. While on the road he was able to travel to different places during the weekend. These were places that were within driving distance of the city in which he was working. Consequently, he saw national parks, Civil War battlefields, Mount Rushmore, and many different sites. This increased his admiration and appreciation for his country and he truly came to understand that America was indeed beautiful and exciting.

Work was also eye opening. He met so many intelligent, innovative, and resourceful capitalists, entrepreneurs, and high-level management people. His admiration and appreciation for these innovative people grew daily. What he learned was these were hard charging but fair people. They competed with each other but were able to appreciate the genius of their competitors. They were also very concerned about how their companies were viewed by the public. Some of their caring was altruistic and some of their caring was because it was good business. They absolutely understood how critical it was that they treated the public fairly and with respect. He had been given the impression these capitalists were greedy, evil, and only interested in exploiting their workers and the public for their own gain. This was a false impression.

He did understand that the capitalist was doing what he was doing to make a profit. The capitalists' performance in the business world was more important to him even than was his performance, when participating in some athletic endeavor. He understood the capitalists' competitive spirit since he would take up their challenge to a game of tennis, paddleball, or handball. They certainly did not take pity on him just because he was a government agent.

Getting away from the business office and competing with these people was also a learning experience. They would relax somewhat and the conversation was less guarded. He learned these capitalists tolerated the agents because they had to. Some of the capitalists even mentioned they could at times learn something. But the capitalist also understood that the role of the agent was to understand all the nuances of the laws and regulations and try to catch him or his staff in a minor violation so the government could extort funds from him above his regular fees and taxes. Theses owners would let him know how they did appreciate some of the agents who believed it was their real function to help the firm serve the public in a safer manner and protect the assets of the public. These capitalists would tell him directly that they knew an agent with that attitude would last with the government for a limited time, because he was not a producer in the eyes of the government.

A few of the agents with whom he worked were fair-minded people. Like him, they thought their real duty should be to assist the capitalist in running a more efficient business so the interest of the public was protected and made safer. When he would work with regional agents, he found less of this attitude and more of an "I caught you, now pay up" attitude. The regional positions were considered the plum positions by most since weekends were always spent at home as were most evenings. The regional agents would generally travel within a day's drive of home. This became very lucrative for the agents since the rule was that only two agents could ride in one vehicle. The regional's would put four to a vehicle and collect the generous government mileage allowance for two vehicles. This was meaningful extra income. All in the Agency knew this was happening. The attitude was "do not tell us, we do not want to know." Besides, they deserve the extra income; it is only government money anyway.

If he had worked in a plum position in a region, he would have become jaded or left the Agency very early. The overall attitudes in the regions were very cynical and anti-capitalist. They would scorn these private business owners, justifying the actions if the Agency because they believed it was the duty of the government to take profits from these evil people anyway they could. Although he did not see it, one of his fellow traveling agents told him how the darling of the Agency had altered a document, and then lied about it, so the government could extort a huge sum from one of the smaller regional institutions. That scoundrel agent was applauded and then promoted because of this action. It made no difference to the Agency that in months the institution filed for bankruptcy and the government had to cover the losses of the public. Although this was the most noted case, other agents had been doing this same thing.

During his tenure with the Agency he saw more and more regulations being issued with which he had questions. It seemed these regulations were less and less about regulating the institutions and protecting the assets of the general public, but they were becoming more and more geared to regulate subjective social justice issues. The institutions were primarily charged with safeguarding the assets of the American public and generating for them a competitive but non-speculative return on the funds the public placed with the institutions. In order to perform this function, the owners had directed their managers and other responsible parties to employ the highest underwriting standards, and always treat any transaction as if they would have to live with that transaction for the life of the transaction. Even if that asset were sold to another institution, the owners believed the asset must represent the highest quality. This attitude had served the owners, the institutions, and the public very well.

One of the early regulations with which he had questions dealt with business transactions. In the past, those in the institutions who would give the final approval to that business transaction, would base approval on proven criteria, such as quality of collateral and anticipated continuance of such quality, the ability of the business to honor its commitment based on objective information such as ability, and willingness to honor those commitments, measured by time honored data verification methods. The regulation stated these time-honored measurements that substantiated the income and safety expected by the institution, could no longer be the only or even the primary measurement. In place of these measurements, the institution must place as its highest criteria, whether they were serving equitably all geographic, social, and economic strata.

The regulations required that the institutions serve businesses in areas where collateral was and had been deemed inferior. If the collateral was in what had been classified as a second, third, or fourth-class location, the collateral must still be valued as if it were in a first class location.

In addition, each borrower must be approved based only on his verbal declarations with no third party verification of any kind. The reasoning for this regulation was so individuals would not be penalized for any past actions, and the assumption that as the business areas were able to grow and improve due to these regulations, all areas would indeed attain first class status within a reasonable period of time.

Within a short period of time another regulation was issued; it said the criteria and standards that had been issued for business transactions, was to be extended to all transactions. The criteria that had been used in the past to measure collateral, ability to repay, and willingness to repay must be ignored. It was deemed by the Agency, at the direction of Congress, that all people, whether citizens or not, were not to be discriminated against for any reason, including financial capability to honor their commitments. The reasoning was that if people were less financially capable then others, it was because they had less access to finances. The regulation stated that as these criteria were implemented, the results would be a more financially equal and socially just society that would result in financial prosperity for all.

He had tried to ask different people in the Agency why this type of financial irresponsibility and social engineering was being forced upon the financial community they were regulating, and would this not end in a financial calamity for all. He expressed that it was putting the capital of the owners at risk and the capital of all Americans. His direct superior told him that with that type of attitude and his constant questioning of why, his days at the Agency could be short- lived. In addition, he was told that he was not finding enough infractions that would generate the required punitive fines on the institutions. The superior went on to inform him it was not his responsibility to assist those evil owners and managers in running safer institutions, but it was his duty to make sure theses evil owners paid their fair share since the tax code allowed them to take advantage of many loopholes. He came away from that meeting understanding that unless he assumed the attitude of the majority of the agents, he would be on the street looking for work.

Within weeks of the conversation with his superior, he had been given an assignment in Jacksonville, Florida. He had been in Jacksonville in the past and, in fact, had been in the very institution designated in this assignment. He had grown to like Jacksonville and had a wonderful experience the last time he was there. He had worked with one of the owners of the institution. He had gained a great deal of respect for that owner and thought the owner felt the same about him.

The first couple of days in any of the assignments were always very busy gathering required information and establishing protocol. He had always tried to establish a working and respectful relationship, understanding the institution still had business to conduct. This was in direct contrast with many of the agents who believed they should be intimidating and demanding. This attitude was in direct contrast to his basic belief that any bureaucrat, elected or unelected, was a servant and the citizen was the ruler. He believed that was what the United States Constitution implied and the Tenth Amendment directly stated.

By the end of the first week and the beginning of the second week, he was to the part of the assignment where he was having daily conversations with the designated representative of the institution. He was fortunate because that designated representative was the same one from the time before; the one with whom he believed he had developed a mutual trust and respect. He learned he was correct in his assessment. During the conversations they would drift from the topic at hand. This was something he had protected against in the past; in fact, he had never allowed it to happen.

The conversation he had with his superior was weighing heavily on his mind. It made him really question if what he was doing was honest work, much less honorable work. It was true he had grained a tremendous amount of knowledge and knew his topic extremely well, but the one area in which he never felt comfortable was playing the "gottcha" game. Now he would be expected to not only become devious or become a liar, but he would be expected to enforce these new regulations. These regulations he believed were wrong and would bring about a major financial crisis, destroying the hard earned savings of Americans who thought he was protecting those very savings.

Late on a Wednesday afternoon --he remembered it was a Wednesday because he always flew home on Thursday afternoon at the end of an assignment -- the discussion with the owner started to drift more than it had previously. They both knew the official business was done, anyway. The owner suggested they continue the conversation off premises. He agreed, and they chose a place some distance from the institution so they would negate the chance of another agent walking in on them. He had never gone to have a private conversation with any institution owner, manager, or employee. He believed this to be unprofessional, even though some of the agents would fraternize with employees of the opposite sex. This was clearly against Agency policy; however it was overlooked, especially if you were bringing many cases of extortion to a satisfactory financial conclusion.

After they had been shown to a private corner and the waitress had brought them their order, the owner asked him if they could have a discussion man-to-man and not agent- to-owner. He did not know exactly what the owner meant. The owner had already clearly established the bill would be split. The owner's clear intent was that this would be a man-to- man meeting and not a business meeting.

Thanking him for his respect and trust, the owner started the conversation by asking him what in the hell he was doing. He asked the owner in his typical fashion as to what the owner was referring and why he would ask the question. The owner said he was referring to him working for the Agency where he clearly did not fit. The owner went on to explain he did not fit for two major reasons, and these were the two most fundamental areas of the work he was doing. The owner said the Agency, and most all agents, acted as tyrants. The owner said those in the industry knew the Agency viewed itself as a tyrannical agency whose sole purpose was to extort funds from the institutions, while putting forth the image to the public it was there to protect the safety of their savings against the evil, greedy capitalist. The owner explained that at institution conferences the different agents were discussed. The agents were put into two categories; those agents who were conniving, underhanded, and held in great contempt, and those who were trying to protect the publics' funds. The owner went on to explain the vast majority of agents fell into the former category with very few falling into the latter. The latter did not last very long at the Agency. The owner also explained that this same majority of agents reveled in the regulations these agents would refer to as socially just regulations that would spread the wealth and bring about a fair and equitable society as defined by Karl Marx.

The owner continued by saying that he fit into the minority group in both situations. The owner than went on to ask again what in the hell he was doing. He was clearly a fish out of water. The owner said the discussion about him at the conferences was one of wonderment as to why he was still with the Agency and how he had lasted so long. The owner told him if he were in any region he would not have lasted a year because he was not a petty tyrant and because he was a capitalist in the truest sense. The owner also explained to him he was not offering him a job because he did not think he would make a good long-term employee. Institutions liked and appreciated employees who would ask why; however they learned truly independent people would leave to start their own business just when they were becoming profitable to the institution.

The owner continued on to explain that he should seriously start to think about what business he might want to start, because based on past experiences, his days with the Agency were surely numbered. The owner suggested to him that he not look for work with any of the other institutions, because during those discussions, all the other owners had also expressed the same reservations he had about hiring him. However, the owner went on to explain, that during those same discussions at the conferences, many of the owners including him, had expressed a real interest in hiring him on a consulting basis. The owner then went on to explain some of the thoughts the owners had expressed as to how that would work.

By that time it was getting late, and after splitting the bill, he thanked the owner for his input. The owner would not be in the next day, so they said their good-byes and went their separate ways. He had a very difficult time sleeping that night and, for the first time in a long time, was unable to concentrate on the book he was reading on the plane the next day. That was a surprise since the book was a study on the different writings of Karl Marx. It was because of his study of Marxism that he had pursued over the last several years, that he found himself in the minority of agents at the Agency and why his life was about to be turned upside down.

CHAPTER 4

It was a long weekend for him. It was one of the few weekends he did not go out with friends or go to some Saturday late afternoon barbecue. He had much to ponder. He knew he would resign from the Agency shortly. But then, what would he do? It was just becoming too difficult and complicated to remain. More and more the new regulations he was supposed to enforce were contrary to his beliefs and contrary to the idea of free enterprise and individualism. The Agency was under more and more pressure to extract funds from the institutions. Consequently, more and more the extraction of funds was becoming the predominant measurement in agent reviews. He was at the bottom all the time. Having always made decisions on his own without consulting family or friends, he argued with himself all weekend. The argument was when to leave and what to do, not if he should or should not resign.

His next assignment was to be in San Diego. When he left for San Diego, he knew he would be staying downtown right across from Coronado Island. San Diego was a city he greatly enjoyed. There was always great weather, and the downtown area was clean and relaxing. The institution in which he would be working was, once again, one in which he had worked previously. He had developed the same type of relationship with the owner in San Diego that he had with the one in Jacksonville. He also knew the two owners knew each other and were, in fact, friends. The plane ride to San Diego was pleasant, and his status with the airline enabled him to fly first class, which was always an added plus.

After the hectic pace of the first couple of days of the assignment, the pace slowed, and he was able to spend some evening time thinking about his situation. The other agents avoided him; to the point he was not even asked if he would like to have dinner with them. This was a blessing since he really was not interested in socializing and hearing the stories of how they would be cleverly extracting funds.

In the second week, when he was meeting with the owner to go over the details of the assignment, the owner mentioned to him that he would like to meet with him after business on Wednesday. The owner mentioned in one of the other meetings he had received a call from his friend in Jacksonville. They had a discussion and the owner thought he would be interested in their discussion. Needless to say the time up until quitting time on Wednesday went very slowly.

He met the owner in a place he knew none of the other agents ever frequented. Again the owner explained this was not a business meeting but a man-to-man meeting and, so, the bill would be split. They were given a booth in a quiet corner, and after the waitress had brought their order, the owner opened the discussion on the topic at hand. The owner repeated some of what he had heard in Jacksonville; things like what the owners discussed at conferences concerning the agents and the Agency. He then confirmed what he had been told by the Jacksonville owner about the owners discussing of the agents and the owners understanding of the real goals of the Agency. The San Diego owner also repeated that the owners were surprised he was still with the Agency and that it was the consensus he would be gone very shortly.

The San Diego owner went on to explain that he and the Jacksonville owner had an idea for him and would share it with him if he was interested and wanted to hear it. He explained that he had a long weekend and this topic was the reason and, yes, he would very much like to hear what the owner had to say. The San Diego owner went on to explain that a common discussion at the institution conferences was how the owners believed an independent consultant who knew and understood the Agency would be of a great benefit. The consultant would have to be a person who was trustworthy, knowledgeable, inquisitive, always would ask why, and who would be reliable. This person would have to commit to visit the institutions on a quarterly basis for a couple of days and be available by other means of communication at other times. He would have to review new formal rulings from the Agency and, also, as much as possible, informal policies and procedures. When these took place, he would have to communicate his findings with the institutions and how the institutions could best deal with the regulations and policies.

For this service, the San Diego and Jacksonville owners said they would be willing to pay handsomely, and knew other owners would, as well. Of course, there would be no employee relationship; it would be strictly a consulting agreement. In addition, the owner explained they could have no formal agreement once he terminated his relationship with the Agency, for 30 days according to the law, but felt it would be in everybody's best interest to wait 60 days. The rest of the evening was spent discussing some of the details the owners had in mind and things he would need to prepare, should he move forward. The final question the San Diego owner asked him is how long it would take him to decide what he wanted to do. He said the decision to leave the Agency had been made weeks ago, but he was just finalizing it in his mind. He believed the decision had been finalized that evening. Over the weekend he would have to go through details, but would probably resign by the end of the month. He was obligated to give two weeks' notice, but had indications once he gave notice, the Agency would not send him on another assignment.

He told the San Diego owner he would keep both he and the Jacksonville owner informed. He would also get started on agreements as they had discussed, and would anticipate beginning his consulting business in about three months. He would also welcome the Jacksonville institution and the San Diego institution as his first clients. In time, they could reveal to him the other institutions they knew wanted to avail them of this service, but felt nothing should be said to anybody else until the resignation and the 30-day period had passed.

The plane ride home from San Diego was too short. He was always able to get so much done on the plane since there were no phone calls or other distractions. He had mastered the art of discouraging chatty people seated next to him; having a book in your face prior to takeoff and early in the flight was critical. Also, avoiding eye contact was important. Employing these proven methods, he was able to get to work and plan his new venture.

He knew he had several weeks of paid vacation coming and, of course, the government paid for sick time not taken, a benefit he had never used. He was not sure if the Agency would treat him like they had treated other people in the past when they had given their notice, by paying them for the two weeks but not sending them on assignment. Typically, the agents would be paid for those two weeks as normal payroll, plus they would receive a lump sum for unused vacation and unused sick leave. This should cover him quite easily for a 90-day period without drawing anything from his savings. Financially he should be fine, even if he did not receive his first check from his new business right at the 60-day mark.

Looking at his schedule, he was to be in New York for his next assignment and Detroit after that. The schedule made the issue of timing very simple. He always enjoyed New York, and he would be in Manhattan, which made the assignment even better. Missing Detroit would be just fine. He also knew another class was being trained and the Agency would be able to cover the Detroit assignment easily. When he thought about the situation, maybe the plan of the Agency was to fire him before, or after, Detroit. He would have to send his letter of resignation after he started the New York assignment and make it official for the end of the Detroit assignment, explaining he wanted to give the Agency adequate advance notice.

After he had made that decision and had done his financial calculations, he started to make his list of things he had to get done. He had to decide on a form of business but would discuss that with his accountant. He had to draft an initial contract and then have an attorney review it. He would have to put together forms for his communications with his clients, talk to some design people, and make sure he had a very reliable computer person that would help him. Initially, he would do everything, and being the type of person he knew he was, this would continue until it was absolutely necessary to hire help.

He also had to put together a marketing plan because he would not just hope that people would call him. He had a commitment from his first two clients, but really needed three more to be financially sound. His rough estimate was that he could do the necessary research, communicate the changes in regulations and policies, answer the individual emails and calls, do the other necessary functions, and do the required travel for six to ten clients without additional people. He would have to do some research to learn what functions he could do by outsourcing and what functions would have to be done in-house. Lists and lists and lists, and now it seemed like so little time to do it all. The final list he made on the plane was a priority list.

What an exciting weekend he had. Of course, the normal functions had to be done like the laundry and cleaning and packing for New York, but rather than doing any socializing, he setup a budget for the time from resignation to anticipated first checks from his new business.

He would not be receiving any per diem after resignation, and so would have much higher living expenses because he would be home. He would have to become a better shopper. He would have higher food bills, gasoline bills, energy bills, and other expenses. He also felt he should, and needed to, take a few days and get away to the Caribbean. Those plans did not have to be made right away.

He decided to compose his letter of resignation on late Saturday afternoon. In his typical fashion he knew it would be a short, maybe two-sentence letter. He decided he would send it to the Agency on the first Friday of his assignment in New York and also fax it to the Human Resources department on that same Friday afternoon. He would show his final day to be the last Friday of the Detroit assignment. That Saturday evening was very relaxing, after the letter had been composed and prepared. He felt a sense of peace he had not felt for a long time. He knew the decision was final. He would not even pretend like he was trying to extract funds from the institutions in Manhattan or Detroit, if the Agency sent him. Never again would he have to try to justify regulations, which were clearly not in the best interests of the safety of the assets of the American public or the institutions, who were responsible for those savings.

He would never again have to enforce those policies to which he was so adamantly opposed; that being executing devious methods to extract funds from the institutions so the government could use those funds for what they called socially-just programs, or forcing the institutions to abandon solid underwriting policies for ones which were drafted for the purpose of social engineering and were endangering the American public's savings and the financial viability of the institutions. Within a very short time, he would be helping the institutions so they could protect the savings of the American public and protect the financial viability of the institutions, which are free and independent American businesses. That night he slept the best he had slept in years. He felt free.

He arrived in New York and met the other agents for the mandatory pre-assignment meeting. He learned he would be working with a group of agents who were always in the top echelons of extracting funds from institutions. The agent, who was in charge of assignments, gave him the most mundane and monotonous assignment of all, even though there were newer and less capable agents on the assignment. The charge agent then went on to explain to all of the agents that it was their duty to extract as much as possible, since the evil capitalist was stealing from the public and the workers. It was the agent's number one duty to be sure the ill-gotten profit was returned to the people, the charge agent said. The charge agent also reminded the agents that all of them were expected to extract, and looked directly at him. He knew this would be a long two weeks. The next couple of days were considered set-up days, so he felt little to no pressure. He also avoided the other agents, both at lunch and after work. On Thursday morning the charge agent found him and asked him, directly, how he was doing and what would they be able to expect next week. He was able to talk around the issue, but knew that meeting with the charge agent was not a spontaneous meeting, but a planned meeting with a purpose.

By noon he had made a decision that he would mail his resignation letter that day and fax it to Human Resources that evening. Late on Friday morning the charge agent told him that the two of them would have lunch, together, because of an important issue. He, of course, knew the important issue.

At lunch the charge agent, after some uncomfortable small talk, told him he had a letter that was faxed that morning and it was for him. He knew what the letter was about, but not the specifics. The charge agent gave it to him and asked him to read it. The letter acknowledged his letter of resignation and stated that his resignation was accepted. The date of resignation he stated was also acceptable. The letter briefly explained that all unused vacation time and unused sick days would be paid. The letter went on to state that it would be in everybody's best interest if he did not go to his assignment in Detroit and that he should also leave for home from New York that afternoon.

He was informed in the letter that he would be receiving a package with all the proper paperwork and details. He should go ahead and review the materials and if he had questions, to contact Human Resources by telephone. The last three weeks' compensation, the letter went on to tell him, would be paid in the normal fashion. When he was done reading the letter, the charge agent asked if he had any questions. Even if he had, he would not have asked the charge agent, so he told him no. The charge agent then told him there was no reason to go back to the institution. The charge agent gave him an itinerary that showed he had a reservation for a flight home late that afternoon. It was clear the charge agent was uncomfortable when he said that the head of the Agency had asked him to express the Agency's gratitude for his effort during the years and for his cooperation in what could have been an uncomfortable situation. The charge agent might not have understood what that statement meant, but he surely did.

On the way back to the hotel to pack, and then on the ride to the airport, he was somewhat nostalgic. He had seen the country, the whole country. He had certainly met some great people in the institutions; people that would be critical to his future. He had even met some agents that he had liked, but none with whom he would continue any type of a relationship. He had also learned how the Agency and other governmental departments were covertly opposed to free enterprise and despised the concept of profit. In private they would explain all business was done for the community and all benefits should be for the community. This he would not miss. This he would now directly and openly oppose.

By the time he landed at his home airport and had taken a cab home, his nostalgic mood had passed, and he was starting to plan the next steps to put together his business. He had been blessed with an extra week he did not expect, and would use that time wisely. He knew the news of his resignation would spread through the institutions quickly, but he must refrain from any direct contact of any kind for at least 30 days after his official resignation date, or almost two full months. It would be three months before he would officially speak with his first two prospective clients.

The next couple of weeks were truly a lesson in patience. He and his accountant determined his business form. He had also decided on a name. All of this had to be registered and papers had to be filed. It required that he go to both County and State offices. This experience easily turned out to be the most frustrating. In all situations he had to stand in line for endless hours. While standing in line, only two or three windows would be open. Other apparent staff would be standing in the back drinking coffee or sodas and talking and laughing. When it was the State or Counties employees break time, they closed their window no matter how long the line was. At one time in the State office, not one window was open for over 30 minutes. When he would finally get to the window, he was met with an arrogant and a condescending attitude. When he asked a question, he was told that he should know since he thought he was so smart that he could start a business.

Despite those obstacles, he was able to get all the paperwork done and took it to his accountant. Now it was time to get started on the fun part. When he got home, he grabbed a new legal pad and his notes, and headed down to the pool area. It was a beautiful day, and because it was a weekday, he knew he would be alone and not be distracted. The first project would be to prepare the agreement so he could take it to the attorney. He had most of the basics on paper, and those that were not on paper were formulated in his mind. This project would be mostly about organizing and arranging. He had set a meeting with his attorney for the Monday of the next week and so he felt comfortable he would be ready.

He had been at his work for quite some time and had been in deep concentration. He was getting thirsty and decided to get a drink, when he noticed this very attractive dark-haired lady smiling at him. He politely greeted her and she responded by asking what had happened that a young lady could not even get noticed. Embarrassed and flustered, he somehow muttered that it had nothing to do with her; he was really concentrating and had a deadline he was trying to meet. He was now going to get something to drink and would bring a drink for her if she would like.

After returning with the drinks, he sat down opposite her and started a conversation. He found he enjoyed talking with her. She seemed very smart, well educated, and quite delightful. He finally asked her what she did that she was able to spend a weekday afternoon by the pool. Rather than answering the question, she responded that she was wondering the same about him. He explained that he had recently resigned his position so he could start a business of his own. She then explained that she had also just resigned her position last Friday and was not sure what she would do. She said she had to give a two-week notice, but her employer said she should just not work those last two weeks. With her accumulated leave time and unused sick pay; she was going to take a week for herself before looking for another position. The idea of starting her own business had never really entered her mind, but maybe it would be a good idea.

He asked her what she had done. She explained she was in the IT department of a government agency who publicly said their function was to protect the savings of the American public but, in reality, they were becoming an entity that would extort funds from the institutions they regulated because the Agency believed the institutions were really stealing form the American public. Last week her supervisor came to her and told her she was being given a new and very important position. This position was to work closely with a couple of their best agents in the field, and that team would develop ways the Agency could use the computer systems to extort even more funds without the institutions having any idea their computers had been hacked. She was told she would be rewarded with a small fraction of a percent of what had been extorted. In total, this would more than double her income.

She went on to explain that she told her supervisor she would have to think about it that evening. As soon as she arrived home she put together her letter of resignation to deliver the next morning. She explained that she had become very unhappy at the Agency, anyway, since she believed the extortion and new regulations that had been passed over the last few years were not about protecting the savings of the American public, but were geared to social engineering and a share the wealth mentality. She then explained she did not mean to become political, but was very concerned as to what was happening in the country. She knew, she said, that she did not want to be an active contributor, but really wanted to find a way to meaningfully oppose and maybe even stop this type of extortion and this attitude.

He wondered if he was being set up. Not knowing for sure, he explained that he really had to get back to work so he would not miss his deadline. And then, because he was very curious about the coincidence and also because he was a young man that was very attracted to this lady, he asked if she would like to have dinner Friday evening. She accepted with the caveat that she would meet him at the restaurant. They arranged a time and place, and he gathered his information and left.

Concentrating the rest of the evening was difficult, but he managed to get much of his work done. He also was able to formulate a plan to check the story of the young lady. He had to speak with a person he had come to know and trust at the Agency. This person was the person with whom he would work to finalize his paperwork and arrange for payment for his unused vacation and sick pay. He did have a couple of questions, but had decided he would not bother her until next week. He adjusted his schedule and called her the next morning. Even though the paperwork did not require it, he asked her if he could meet with her that afternoon or the next morning. They agreed on a meeting the next morning before her work at a little coffee place near her office.

It was another restless evening. He did not remember when he had hoped for a certain outcome of a meeting that he knew was about a person he had just met. If her story were true, the lady at Human Resources would certainly be aware of what had happened. Typically, he would never have lost sleep because he was planning how to approach a subject. He had become quite adept at getting information over the last several years, but he really wanted to be more direct at the meeting the next morning. Right before the meeting he still had not decided on his approach.

He met the HR lady at the coffee shop where they were able to find an isolated booth. After the order had been brought, he quickly went over the business questions he had. The answers were also very quick. When this charade had been completed, the HR lady looked at him and said that before he got to his real purpose for wanting to meet, she had some news that might interest him. The two of them had grown to trust each other over the years. She had become a mother-like figure to him. The HR lady then went on to describe a situation that had taken place the week before. The situation the HR lady described was the exact details of the story he had heard the day before from the attractive dark-haired lady. The HR lady said that she had always intended to introduce the two of them, but the opportunity had never presented itself. She went on to explain she knew both of them were having difficulties adapting to the changes that had been taking place in the Agency and she knew both of them were either going to resign or be fired. She believed the supervisor who went to the attractive lady with the proposition, went with the intent to force her resignation just like his set up in New York had been to force his resignation. The Agency did not want to fire either of them, because they believed there would be very negative repercussions.

The HR lady then asked him what his real reason for asking to meet her was. He smiled and told her she had just answered his question. He then explained the strange coincidence that had taken place the previous day. They both had a pleasant laugh. He asked the HR lady what she could tell him about the young lady without breaking any protocol. His mother- like figure answered in a mother-like way, explaining how much she had grown to admire the young lady. She explained the young lady was extremely capable, a very good and hard worker, and possessed impeccable standards. If she, his mother- like figure could pick someone for him, she would pick that attractive dark-haired young lady. It was time to leave, but before they parted this mother- like person to him insisted that she be kept in-formed of what took place business wise and personally.

He nearly danced down the street to his car. He was very anxious for Friday evening. He anticipated this date more than any he could remember. But all that had to be put aside because he still had much to do. He was able to put the agreement together so he would be ready for the attorney on Monday morning. Now he had to start developing a marketing program along with the details of the business. This included organizing his communications with his clients and creating full research developing plans for aiding the institution in combating the tactics of the agency. Much of this was computer based. This was his real weakness and where he became easily frustrated.

Friday evening finally arrived and, as usual, he arrived twenty minutes early. She arrived right on time and to him, she was absolutely beautiful. Based on the looks of the other men and some women in the restaurant, he was not the only one who thought she was beautiful. He really enjoyed the jealous looks of the men when she walked up to him and gave him a little peck on the cheek. Dinner proved to be very interesting as well as enjoyable. He had decided he would change the topic or avoid as much as possible talking about his plans.

He learned that she had a very different upbringing from what he had. She was the only child of a military man and his wife. Much of her childhood was spent overseas with the bulk of that time in Germany. She took advantage of the opportunities under the tutelage of her father and mother. They made sure she learned history, and she saw the places where much of that history actually occurred. Having been introduced to history early in life, she also grew into a history student, mostly of Western European history.

Their mutual interest in history led them eventually to the person of Karl Marx. He learned she had also studied the life and teachings of Marx. They both held the same view that the ideas of Marx had never and, could never work. She concurred that the idea that all productive property should be controlled by a central entity, and that all of the ideas of the people should conform to the ideas of the state, can only be implemented in a totalitarian state. He also learned that she was well aware that the American people did not understand Marxism and that many of the ideas of Marxism were starting to take hold in the United States. The conversation moved on to other more personal topics and before they knew it, it was very late.

As they were preparing to leave, she asked him why he had avoided talking about his business plans. Of course, he thought she had not noticed. Somewhat embarrassed, he explained that, yes, he had avoided it, but since it was so late they would have to set up another time to discuss it. She smiled and said that would be a wonderful idea, but was sure he would want to discuss it in a less public place, so maybe he should come over to her place late Sunday afternoon for a glass of wine and a light dinner. After exchanging phone numbers so he could get the location of her apartment in the large complex, he walked her to her car and said good night with a hug and a kiss on the cheek. Neither mentioned the fact that they had limited their discussion about their families.

On Saturday he called his mother-like figure to tell her about the dinner date and to explain he and the dark-haired lady were meeting on Sunday to specifically talk about what he would be doing. The HR lady did not know the details of his plans, which he could not tell her for her own protection, but he wanted assurance one last time that it was safe to be completely open with this enchanting dark- haired young lady. The HR lady assured him the new lady in his life could be totally trusted. Not only could she be trusted, but also she was the best the Agency had in the IT department. The HR lady then played the role of the mother-like figure and added that he would be a fool if he weren't more interested in her as a woman than as a person to help him with his business. He thanked his mother-like figure for the advice and assured her, his interest was in the proper place.

He knew he could not be twenty minutes early on Sunday, but he knocked on her door right on time. Conversation was very easy and natural. After a glass of wine and a light dinner, he asked if she was ready for him to go into business mode and explain what he had in mind. She was very attentive, not interrupting to give advice, but only to ask questions. He gained more and more admiration for her because these questions were insightful and showed just how much she understood and how astute she was. Before long they were discussing and planning. Her insights on organizing the communications and research, as well as ideas on how he could be of even more help to the institutions, were remarkable. Quickly, it was very late, and they both knew there was so much more to discuss. Prior to his leaving he asked her if she would be willing to work with him over the next several weeks, organizing his business and preparing for his opening.

She said of course, but it would have to be on an as-available basis since she would have to start looking for another position. He assured her he would pay her for her efforts and time, but it would have to be done on a deferred basis, and they would have to reach an agreement, soon. He also made sure she understood he wanted to continue to see her socially, as well, and with a smile she explained that would be wonderful. The business plan was that she had enough information to begin doing some preliminary work, and they would check with each other on an as-needed basis. Friday night, however, would be set-aside for a date with no business discussed.

Over the next several weeks the business plan took form. The business discussions became more like discussion between business partners. The social meetings developed into a warm and trusting romance. With growing understanding of each other, their respect and admiration grew each day. She started to assume certain duties and developed much of how the business would function.

Eight weeks after the day he faxed his resignation, he had contact with the owners of the institutions in Jacksonville and San Diego. They both agreed to become clients and said they would sign the agreements on the 61st day after the effective date of his resignation. The owner of the San Diego institution, who was also the current president of the institutions association, asked him if he would be willing to be the key note speaker at the association's annual meeting in three months. The association would also like him to do a workshop explaining how his business could benefit the association's members. The association would compensate him very nicely, and he could have a spot with other vendors.

The San Diego owner told him he had a list of six other institutions that had contacted him and told him they knew about this new business and wanted to become clients as quickly as they could. The owner said he would email the information to him.

This would give him eight clients the first week he opened his business and shortly, thereafter, he would be presenting to the association. He was jubilant and could not wait to call her to share this news. After the initial part of the telephone call, which was filled with laughter and joy, she told him they had much to plan and he should come over to her place because she had the marketing and business plans on her computer.

CHAPTER 5

He gathered some materials he thought would be important and started the short walk to her place. Even in his wildest dreams, he had not allowed himself to believe the start could be so good. He had hoped to have maybe two additional clients, for a total of five. This would have allowed him to ask her to work as a contractor for him at about 80% of what she had been earning at the Agency. It would have allowed him to pay himself at the same 80% of what he had been earning. He had hoped that within a couple of months he would be able to increase both of them to 100% of their Agency earnings, and then move up from there. Now he needed her because the workload would be too great for just him, and she was developing systems on the computer that he would have to spend many hours learning. He knew what he wanted to do and now what he had to do.

When she answered his knock on the door, he was greeted with that gorgeous smile and then a very welcoming hug and kiss. He thought she might be even happier than he. She had a couple of glasses of wine poured, and they sat down giggling and smiling like two teenagers. Her first statement was a simple question asking him how he would be able to handle the business alone. He said he would not be able to do it alone, and would need some help, but had no idea where to go to get the competent help he would need. After a few minutes of this flirtatious banter, they decided as much fun as it was, it was time to get serious.

It was obvious he could not handle the workflow alone, and still be able to meet the expected demands of the new clients. They both knew what an opportunity it was to have him as the keynote speaker, conduct a workshop, and have a vendor's booth at the institutions' annual meeting that was to be held in Vancouver that year. He already had an idea as to what he would suggest. He went over projected income and expense numbers with her. At eight fulltime clients, the business could easily afford to pay both of them 100% of what they had been earning, plus cover the payroll costs and health insurance. The accountant had suggested to him that he be a 1099 employee and any outside help he needed, be treated as contract help or 1099 employee for the first year as. He had planned on leaving any profit in the business, for now, and she agreed with him.

After they had worked through those details, she looked at him and told him that depending on how many clients would sign agreements with him initially, she was planning on submitting her resume to him. She said she did not remember when she had been so involved in a project, and she knew it was the work, and not just working with him. She now understood completely, what the Agency was doing pushing its "Marxist" ideas. She knew what they were doing was very important. This idea, she said, of social engineering and extorting the profits from the institutions that were needed to help expand the American economy for the good of all, should not be taken by the government to be given as handouts for the real purpose of buying votes. She went on to say she could not think of any work she could do that was more important and then, smiling, added or work with someone she respected and admired more.

The plan they designed that evening, and the next morning over breakfast, was that he would continue to put together the materials he would need for his first meetings with the institutions then, and for the next several months. In addition, he would contact the other six institutions to arrange to get them started on the 62nd day, as opposed to the 61st day. He would also have to start to put together the talk he would be giving at the annual conference. They agreed they should both present at the workshop, and both should be prepared to work the booth. It was very interesting how they both just took for granted that she would also go to Vancouver and be an intricate part of their overall presentation. As the time grew nearer, she took it upon herself to make the airline reservations and book the hotel.

A conscious decision was made that any new agreements beyond the eight would not be signed until after the annual meeting. The time between the start date and the annual meeting would be used to work through any unforeseen situations and to put a workable routine in place. Although things did flow smoothly, as could be expected, there were a few areas that needed to be adjusted, plus it was good for them to get comfortable with the flow. It was important that their current clients not have to say, "Things were good, but." It is always that "but" that prospective clients wanted to have explained. By the time they were taking a taxi to the airport, they knew their present clients would give glowing reports, if asked, and would volunteer glowing reports, if not asked.

They were also excitedly anticipating the reactions when he would announce at his keynote speech a new computer program that had been developed which would enable the institutions to combat the recent program the Agency had developed to extort even more funds. She had been able to learn of this program and the Agency had just started to use it. Once she learned who had designed it and what it was intended to do, she was able to design a program to combat the Agency without the Agency even knowing they had been detected. The program had been tested in the Jacksonville Institution, and the results were better than even she expected.

He received a very enthusiastic, standing ovation after his address on the first evening of the meeting. He introduced her to the group and explained she had written the program to combat the Agencies new scheme and it would be her role to implement and maintain that program. She was also warmly greeted. Both were bombarded with questions after the meeting was adjourned. They did not accept any of the many invitations they received to have a nightcap, as they had decided earlier they would retire early and allow the institution owners to speculate on their own.

They learned the next that morning the other workshop that was scheduled opposite theirs had been postponed, and their workshop had been moved to a larger room. They had to get set up for the workshop, as well as get the vendors booth ready.

The workshop was filled to capacity. He opened the workshop and went over some necessary material on how to combat some recently passed regulations. He also talked about some anticipated regulations that would limit profits by requiring the institutions to turn over profits above a certain percentage, to a central government committee, who would then distribute these funds to borrowers who were delinquent for any reason. He then introduced her. She explained what the Agency was doing and how the institutions could combat this new method of extortion. The Agency was creating what they considered an undetectable bug in the institutions computer system by hacking into the system of the institution. The agents would do the necessary preparation when they were in the institution and then, on the next visit, would find these major abuses. The anticipated amounts that would be required by the Agency to settle the abuses would dwarf anything the Agency had extorted to date.

After her presentation, she was bombarded with owners asking her questions. He had slipped out of the room prior to her close and went to the booth. They signed an additional ten full contracts that day. In addition, they signed twenty agreements for the software they had packaged to negate the new program of the Agency. She would give these new clients telephone support. They had an additional ten full contract institutions they had to postpone until the next quarter.

The next morning was very busy answering more questions, arranging calendars, and finalizing details. They had to rush to get everything packed and catch a taxi to the airport for their scheduled flight home. Wisely, she had booked a first class ticket for her and an M class ticket for him, knowing he would be upgraded. They arranged with a kind elderly gentleman to swap seats so they could sit together. Before the wheels were off the ground, she was asleep. He grabbed a book he had wanted to read for some time. He considered the book recreational reading. It was a book written by a Marxist supporter extolling the virtue of a conforming and classless society. The author was trying to show why this system was really best. The book said the system had never worked the way it was intended; in fact, the author said he knew it had always failed. The author went on to explain the failure was not due to the misguided policies of Marxism, but it was due to the mistakes of those who were in charge of its implementation. He knew she would want to read this book, as well, and would give it to her when he had finished. They both preferred to read books written by the supporters of Marx, as opposed to those who opposed his ideology. They both understood the reasons for opposing, but they wanted to understand how those who believed in this philosophy rationalized their belief.

They were both very busy and involved in their different functions of the business. He was able to get agreements signed and services started with the new clients. She was able to get the computer software started in the different institutions. She decided it was best if she traveled to the different institutions, which were using her software. It was worth it to have a personal relationship and also to explain some of the finer details in person. It proved to be a very good decision in the long run, saving her a substantial amount of time and frustration.

They maintained the discipline of separating their relationship and work. When they were having a work meeting, it was kept to work as much as possible. When they were on a date or were spending relationship time, they were disciplined and maintained the time as relationship time. It really was not that difficult since they found each other to be interesting and enjoyed each other's sense of humor, even though others might not.

They had been in business for a little over a year, and all was moving forward. They were able to solve the little details that might come along. Her initial work had paid off putting together a well thought out and very functional way of streamlining the regular business. He was efficient when traveling and was able to effectively meet the schedules and commitments the business had made to the institutions. They did start to hear rumblings that the Agency had heard about their venture. In his private talks with his mother-like figure, it was hinted that their venture had become a topic of discussion at the Agency. The institutions had been able to reduce the amount extorted by at least 50%. The special program the Agency had developed to hack the institutions software had been implemented about a year ago. The expected results to the Agency were just not materializing. When the agents went back into the institutions, the abuses they were supposed to find did not appear. He was told the Agency had made it their primary objective to find out why.

The Agency was also learning that the institutions were finding effective ways around the regulations the Agency had instituted, which were designed to "spread the wealth" and "socially engineer" by forcing the institutions to extend terms to those who did not have adequate collateral, the means to repay, or even had demonstrated the willingness to repay. The Agency did not care that this made the savings of the American public safer by strengthening the capital structure of the institutions, thus, enabling the American economy to grow. That was not the intent of the Agency, and they were not happy their intent was not being accomplished.

It was time for the institutions' annual meeting. The Board had specifically chosen Vancouver for the conference the year before, because they wanted it to be held out of the country. The association was small enough so they knew all who attended, and the association wanted to take every precaution they could, to be sure they were not bugged or did not have unwelcomed Agency personnel snooping around the hotel. The plan had been successful in Vancouver. Because of that success, they decided this meeting would be held in Cologne, Germany. Cologne is a smaller German city on the lovely Rhine River. It is a beautiful old German city that still had some Roman ruins. The Board had found an exquisite older hotel with excellent facilities on the opposite bank of the Rhine from the main historical area, where the famous and beautiful cathedral was located. The public transportation system in Cologne was excellent and made access to the different areas of the city very simple. More importantly, it made it easier for the Board to hold the meeting away from the prying eyes of the Agency. After securing the site, the Board had commented, what a sad commentary it is that they, such an important part of the American economy, had to be concerned about their government spying on them, so the government could find more and better ways to extort funds from them and endanger a huge part of Americans savings, thus, endangering the whole American economy.

She had once again made the reservations for them to attend the conference. They would have a booth in the vendors' area and would be conducting a workshop. This time the Board did not schedule another workshop at the same time. Preparing for this workshop was more difficult than it was to prepare for the one the previous year. They really had to prioritize material, since they would have only 90 minutes to present. She had made some changes to the software, especially since the Agency was continually trying to learn why their hacking was not working.

Also, the Agency had just announced they were forming a new so-called consumer protection board. The Board's function would be to find ways to stop the institutions from taking action to foreclose on the collateral when a default had occurred. The reasoning was that it was not the fault of the consumer that he had to default; it was the fault of the institution because it was the institution that extended the terms to the borrower. The Agency went on say the consumer should not lose his collateral, even though the Agency, a division of the government, had forced the institution to extend the terms. It made no sense to a rational person. One part of the government said the institution had to extend terms, regardless of the ability to repay or the credit worthiness of the customer, and the other governmental branch was saying that the institution knew, or should have known, that the likelihood was that the customer would default at the time the terms were extended and, therefore, could not foreclose on the collateral.

A couple of weeks prior to leaving for the annual meeting of the institutions, she told him she had cleared his schedule for the four days following the meeting in Cologne. She informed him that he should not schedule anything for that time. She told him they were extending their stay in Germany and would be taking a riverboat down the Rhine River and then down the Moselle River to Trier, Germany. Trier is the birthplace of Karl Marx. Marx was raised in Trier. He met his wife Jenny, in Trier. Trier is one of the oldest cities in Germany and was founded by the Romans. She told him she remembered the Rhine and Moselle Valleys were beautiful. He said he thought that would be a great idea, but did not know if he could do it. Of course, she was hurt by his remark and told him that was just fine, he did not have to come along, but she was going. He started to smile and said that he really did not want to take a trip like that with a girlfriend, but had always thought it would be best to do with a fiancé or a wife.

They decided they would get married the next weekend and travel to Germany as a married couple. They could also announce their new partnership to those who had become not only their clients, but also their friends. So far as the business was concerned, it had been operating as a true joint venture. It would now be made a legal joint venture with her owning 50% and him owning 50%. The day they left for Germany they were husband and wife and legal business partners. Both were very happy.

They flew to Amsterdam and then took a short flight to the Bonn/Cologne Airport. She was quickly reminded of autobahn driving from the airport to the city. It did not take long for her to start to understand German again. The short trip into Cologne also brought her back to her childhood; the good times and the bad. Her mother had been killed in one of the horrendous accidents that occur when people drive at those high speeds for which the autobahn is infamous. She had just turned thirteen at the time of the accident and it took a long time for the pain to dull. She and her father went back to the United States shortly thereafter. Her father never really recovered and died while she was in her second year of college. He knew this was painful for her, even though she had assured him she would be fine.

When they arrived at the hotel, the excitement of being greeted by friends and business acquaintances helped her forget the ride into the city. Then one of the ladies spotted her ring finger and all the hugging and congratulations began. The owner of the San Diego institution and his wife insisted on Champagne for all. She only regretted at that time that neither her mother nor father was there to share in the joy.

The meeting was very interesting. Their workshop was successful and they added more clients. They were able to spend more time at the booth talking with clients and prospects then they had in Vancouver. In the last couple of weeks, they had heard the agents were treating the employees of the institutions in a much more aggressive manner, almost hostile. The owners had gathered that the agents were under a great deal of pressure. As the institutions became more aggressive and more successful in fighting and negating most of the funds demanded by the Agency, the pressure on the agents had apparently become intense. In frustration, the agents were combative when their old tricks were no longer working and, obviously frustrated, when the traps they thought they had set by hacking the institutions software never occurred.

The owners also were aware of the agents' frustration when the institutions were able to counteract the negative affect of the most anti-capitalistic regulations of the Agency. Rumors were rampant that the director of the Agency had gone to some of the openly declared Marxist/Progressive members of Congress to inform them of the dilemma the Agency was facing. The facts were very clear. Over the last year, extorted funds had decreased drastically, and the safety of the American public's savings had increased, as had the financial strength of the institutions. Congress, the Administration, the Agency and the America public should have been pleased with such news, but only the American public, who had savings, were pleased.

The two of them and the institutions understood why this was happening. They realized that the effort to bring the institutions and the entire financial industry under the control of a central authority, and, in effect, have a state monopoly as outlined by Karl Marx, would not go away quietly. The hatred of profit, of achievement, of private ownership of productive property, and the desire to have all citizens conform in a classless society where compensation was based on need and not effort was great. Many of the bureaucrats, members of Congress, and the liberal and progressive factions of the American public held this belief. So even though all could celebrate at this meeting, everybody knew the victory for a free capitalist economy had not been won. They would have to remain very diligent.

The cruise down the Rhine and the Moselle was very pleasant and relaxing. They enjoyed the castles, the villages and towns, and the beautiful scenery. They found Trier absolutely fascinating, but then they realized it was more fascinating to them then it would be to most people, because of the history. They saw where Marx lived, where he went to school, and where he would take walks with his future father-in-law. They also saw where Jenny, the future Mrs. Marx, lived as well.

They were well rested when they returned home and were ready to get back to work. She started to feel sick shortly after they arrived home and thought she might have caught something. She felt exhausted all the time, but knew she had much to do, so was a good trooper. It was only a short time before she began to realize the reason for her sickness. Both were very happy and knew some adjustments in the business and their lifestyle would have to take place.

Nine months after their return home, she gave birth to a baby boy. Within a couple of years that little boy would have a sister. The business continued to do well and grow. They were able to run the business, successfully and only added one more person. His mother-like figure from the Agency had told him she was unable to continue at the Agency, and he immediately asked her if she would join them. They not only hired an excellent competent employee, but their children had a grandmother-like figure.

Financially they had invested wisely, and although they enjoyed nice things, they did not waste money foolishly. By this time all of the institutions were using some or all of their services. Their business had become an integral part of the industry. Some of the owners of the institutions had discussed among themselves how critical their business had become to the industry and what would happen if either of them would suddenly be gone. This discussion had become even more important because of what was taking place in Congress and the Agency. Many of the members of Congress were publicly talking about how the Agency was failing the American people. These members were claiming it was the duty of the Agency to limit the profits of the institutions, because the profits really belonged to the community, and not the private owners. Congress members also stated that it is the function of the institution to be sure all Americans were granted terms, and not just those who had collateral, means to repay, and willingness to repay. These Congress members were saying the only function of the institution was to provide terms for the purposes of social engineering, social justice, and, yes, sharing the wealth with all.

These Congress members were calling for a new director of the Agency. These same Congress members said the Agency needed a director who understood the importance of community and was able to counter the efforts of the institutions in combating the wishes of Congress. The

Congress members also began to mention that an evil business, clearly referring to their business, was suspected of aiding the institutions and; thus, collaborating with the evil capitalists in their unlawful action of exploiting the American public for the financial benefit of a few.

The rumors were rampant as to who would be appointed director of the Agency. Recent appointments to other government agencies gave the institutions, as well as the two of them, a good indication. The IRS, the EPA, HHR, Education, The Labor Relations Board and the recently enacted Consumer Protection Agency all had people from academia appointed. Not one of these appointees had come from the private sector. Not one had run a business. All had worked for the government, been a professor at a liberal university, or both. All had written and/or spoken about the evils of the capitalists and how their greed was responsible for all problems. They all had stated in writing, or public talks, that all elements of production must be centralized and all proceeds of labor must be centralized and shared, fairly, by all with a guaranteed minimum income. This would enable people to work at the type of work that gave them individual fulfillment, even though that work was not economically productive. He and she knew these were all direct quotes of Karl Marx. They had learned that very few other Americans knew this. The press was calling this social justice that would bring about a fair and equal society. Many Americans bought into this idea.

When the name of the person who would be appointed director of the Agency was revealed, it was far worse than they had ever imagined. The woman who was named to be director of the Agency was, of all things, a Doctor of Sociology. She had never been associated in any way with business, nor, as far as anyone knew, had any understanding of economics. She had authored several books extolling what she called the social virtues of the Russian Revolutions of 1905 and 1917. She had also written a book on the positive social advances brought about by Mao.

She was praised by the Marxist/Progressives in the Senate, and was proclaimed to be a revolutionary thinker who would establish a socially and financially equitable society through her fair and sensible approach. The institutions called an emergency meeting of their association's board, and both he and she were requested to attend. Every institution would be under a direct threat, along with the American economy, and the American way of life.

CHAPTER 6

The meeting was held the very next weekend. Everybody was in the hotel by noon and was ready to meet, starting at one sharp. The mood was not festive like it had been at the meeting in Germany. The fears these people had about their country, in general, were now very specific, fears that affected them very directly. They knew the American public was not at all aware of the threat they faced. The board must remain sensible, and they must put together a blueprint they could follow. If they did not, they knew a devastating financial crash would certainly take place within the next ten years. They hoped they were realistic and not overly optimistic with that timetable.

He and she knew it would take the new Agency director months for final confirmation after the inevitable appointment was formally made. Some of the powerful opposition on the Senate committee had told the Board president that they could delay the appointment for, realistically, six months. That same delay had taken place with the appointments to the other agencies, but the end result would be the same.

The appointee would be voted out of committee and, once on the floor, would be comfortably approved by the entire Senate. It was reasonable to believe the institutions had one year to prepare for what would be an onslaught of damaging regulations. She told the Board they could expect the new director to hire a group of the finest hackers the new director could find. The Marxist/Progressives in the Senate had expected the amount of extorted funds to go much higher and, instead, those extorted funds had dropped to just a trickle. The new director would have no limit on her budget to correct, what the Marxist/Progressives considered a major wrong. She knew she would not be able to counter the group of hackers she expected.

He knew the efforts to enforce the regulations that the Agency had imposed would be intensified. He also knew that the Agency would involve the Department of Justice to bring suit against the individual institutions, as well as to bring action against the industry as a whole. Although it would be difficult for many of the regulations to become law by passing both Houses of Congress, the Agency, with the backing of the Administration, would consider the regulations to be law and use all the resources available to enforce them. The funds needed by the institutions to fight these actions would be considerable.

All the Board members concurred with these assessments. Before adjourning late that afternoon, the Board decided on the agenda for the next day. In the morning they would discuss other major areas of threat to them. Then, in the afternoon, they would start to formulate a plan to best confront the Agency. They had all anticipated this happening, so would not be unprepared. Several of them had "what if" discussions in the past year. The subject had been briefly discussed in Germany. He and she had been brought into many of these discussions, both in Germany and since. The owners of the Jacksonville and San Diego institutions had scheduled a dinner with them, for that evening, which would be held in a private room.

The four of them, at dinner, quickly recapped the meeting that afternoon. The owners asked her what she thought would be needed, realistically, to continue to thwart the efforts of the hackers in the Agency. Having anticipated this question, she had made some estimates. She explained it would not take a huge staff of programmers, but it would take some very competent programmers. She explained the Agency would hire a huge number of hackers, because that is the way the government worked. She estimated, based on the staff they now had, the Agency would want to at least double their staff, to approximately thirty. Most of them would be incompetent and be more concerned with surfing the web when they thought nobody was looking.

Having worked in this type of atmosphere, she understood the mentality. She also knew that success was based on proficiency and not numbers. Based on this knowledge, she told the owners it would require, at the most, five very good programmers to be able to continue to stay ahead of the Agency. She also said it might be necessary for a programmer to go into an institution for a few days after the agents had left. This way the programmers would be able to keep pace with any changes and effectively negate the hackers' efforts. She could not imagine that the group of five would need any more than two efficient staff people to work with them. She added, as she and he had discussed, that they did not have the resources for a staff of this size and competency.

The owners then asked him to give them an estimate of what additional staff he would need. Having prepared, as well, he explained that it would be best if four experienced lawyers were added to combat the Agency. The attorneys would need a research team of perhaps six people and other necessary office staff. He went on to explain that a decision would have to be made if attorneys would be hired in-house to fight the inevitable lawsuits brought by the Agency and the DOJ, or if it would be better to have a law team on retainer. Under either scenario, he did not have the resources for the appropriate staffing.

The owners told them they concurred with their assessments and had also understood they did not have the resources to hire the appropriate staff. They also understood the staff would have to be hired, soon, and yet they would not be able to raise their fees to support that staff for at least twelve months and, more likely, eighteen months. The institutions could not take the chance however, to allow them to operate as they had without hiring and preparing because that would be certain death for the institutions.

The owners than asked both of them if they believed they could ever be employees again.

Both of them had also anticipated that question and had given it serious consideration. Both he and she explained they might be able to do it for a short period, knowing there was a definite ending.

The owners explained they had a proposal to run by them, understanding, the full Board had not been informed, and the proposal was subject to the full board's approval. With that caveat, the two owners continued to explain what they had in mind. The Board would establish a corporation. This could be done very quickly; in fact, a shell had already been formed. The corporation would be funded and owned by the institutions. The purpose of the corporation would be to provide the services the two of them had been providing, except with the anticipated enhancements.

The Board would authorize the corporation to purchase their business. The value would be based on agreed-upon standards for similar transactions. The agreed upon amount would be paid to them in any manner they wished; that is, cash up front, or spread over some time period, for tax purposes. That decision would be theirs. In addition, the corporation would hire them as employees with an employment contract for two years, at an income of twice what the market would demand. Their duties would be to continue to run the business and provide the services they were providing now, plus they would begin immediately to build the best and most competent staff available. They would also train the staff and direct them. However, in the last six months of the employment contract, they would begin to act more like consultants so the new staff could begin to operate independently of them, and under the direction of the Board appointed CEO of the corporation. They would then be on a consulting contract for three additional years at a substantial income for both of them. The duties would continually lessen over that three-year period, and, in the last year, they would only be on call on an as-needed basis. Plus, they would be expected to attend the quarterly board meetings.

The owners explained they did not expect an immediate answer; however, they would like to have breakfast with them, so they could determine a course of action to be taken for the last session, that afternoon. The rest of the dinnertime was spent in general give-and-take about the direction the industry was taking, the effect on the institutions directly, how best to combat the Agency, and the proposal that was made that evening. None of the four was of the mentality that they liked to hear them talk, so much was accomplished.

It was still relatively early when the dinner ended, and they went directly to their room. There was much to review. It was a review because this very situation had been a topic of conversation between them, over the last month. They had realized what would have to be done. They were both very astute and thought something of this nature would be proposed. The good news was that it was more generous than they had hoped it would be, and the better news was that their commitment time was less than they had anticipated. She already had programmers in mind that she would like to approach, and he had a number of attorneys he knew who would be excellent in the role. The answers they did not have was on what basis the business should be valued, and if they would want the proceeds all upfront, or spread over time. They would have to consult with their accountant.

They decided they would sleep on the matter and see how they felt in the morning. Both anticipated a restless night but, surprisingly, both went to sleep quickly and slept soundly. The next morning they felt comfortable, almost anxious to tell the owners they were ready to have the full Board informed about the plan, understanding some details still needed to be put in place. They were ready for their breakfast meeting almost forty- five minutes early, and were able to have some relaxing discussion time. He told her he really was ready to move on and do something different, but had not decided what that might be. She said she was in the same position, except she had an idea about what they might do. She said for the last several months this idea kept coming back to her. The feeling kept getting stronger and stronger as the conditions in the country kept deteriorating. She continued on explaining that their study of history, along with their study of the philosophy and teaching of Karl Marx, seemed to have put them in a unique position. She had noticed, in speaking with Americans from all political spectrums and social and economic strata, none of them understood what Marx really taught. She thought this was one of the reasons Americans did not understand what was happening in the country; that, and an incredible attitude of indifference.

They met the owners at an isolated table for the breakfast meeting. The Jacksonville owner, again, took the lead and explained that he and the San Diego owner had met for a time, after the dinner meeting ended. The Jacksonville owner said they had gone over the dinner discussion, again, including the proposal that was made, and the two owners felt very good about it. The two owners had not changed their minds overnight, and were wondering what they thought. He explained they liked and were in favor of the proposal, and felt very comfortable having it presented to the whole board that afternoon, understanding details would have to be agreed upon, later. They did not foresee any complications. One of the details would have to be at what time, and under what conditions, would they be able to begin to pursue other interests. They were not ready to divulge to the Board, or anybody, at this time, what those other interests might be. They had not, by any means, made a decision; they only had an idea.

Within thirty days, they were no longer the owners of the business they had started. They knew it was necessary. They also knew they had a big role to play over the next twelve to eighteen months, at which time they believed they would have some time for themselves to sort through the details of what they wanted to do next. In the meantime, they had to start implementing the plan the Board had set forth. That plan included running the business and preparing for the growth of the staff.

She was fortunate. The people she had in mind to bring onboard were nearby and had Agency experience, as well as hacking and programming experience. Within a couple of months, she had half of her staff on board. This enabled her to free herself, somewhat, from the day-to-day operations so far as programming was concerned. She was able to concentrate on filling the rest of the programming staff and to look for competent office staff.

He was not as fortunate, since many of the people he had in mind were not from the immediate area. The Board did not believe it was a deal killer if the attorneys did not live in or near the city, but it would require extra travel and extra time away from home for them. The Board had also decided they would find a firm they would put on retainer for the legal battles. This seemed to make the most sense because they did not know how soon those suits would start or how many there would be. This took some pressure off him, and by the end of the first year, he had his staff in place. Now it would be training, but based on the quality of staff he and she had hired, that would be enjoyable.

As anticipated, the sociologist was approved to become director of the Agency. Her directorship was effective nine months to the day the corporation became owner of the business. This time period was a little longer than they had anticipated. However, the new director started to wield influence much quicker than they had anticipated. Her first area of attack was in the monetary area. As head of the department, she put all her efforts and influence into the hacking project. The mandate Congress gave her was to raise the level of extorted funds to the levels they were at their pinnacle, and then build from there.

The new director was not timid and proclaimed a full onslaught against the institutions. The crews of agents were halved when going into the institutions, and their only function was to extort funds. They did not even pretend to examine for compliance with regulations. The Marxist/Progressives in Congress had stated it was the duty of the Agency to return the funds that were stolen by the institutions through manipulation and deceit, and return this wealth to the people. The capitalists, they declared, did not earn their wealth, but stole it and must return it. The press proclaimed the new director to be the savior of the middle class, who was restoring economic and social justice to the exploited.

This kept the programming staff very busy. The work had been doubled. The staff was able to undo what the agents had done very quickly, but the staff knew they would be facing a greater challenge soon. It was within a short time the corporation faced their first lawsuit from the Agency. The Agency's suit said it was illegal for the corporation's staff to enter the physical premises of the institutions for any reason. The lawsuit claimed that all property, including real estate owned by the institution, was, in fact, the property of the people or the government, and the Agency as the designated regulator, had the right to determine who was and was not trespassing. The Agency further stated that this control was an implied extension of the licensing process.

The reasoning the Agency used had been used by other governmental agencies, as well. It had been used in California recently and upheld by the California Supreme Court. The EPA had recently filed a suit using similar reasoning on private property. The property was a residence and not used in any commercial manner. The EPA claimed their right of ownership came through the extension of their responsibility to protect the air and the water for all, and the intent to build a home on that particular site would endanger both the air and water of the general public despite the appropriate zoning. A judge had ruled that the case had merit and could be brought.

The Agency director had brought on an assistant director for the sole purpose of writing regulations. The new assistant director had also taught sociology at one of the liberal elite schools in the east. The assistant director had stated in many articles, and in many different addresses, that the financial industry should be under the direct control of the people or the government. The assistant director had stated all credit extensions should be granted through such a monopoly. This would be the granting of all real estate loans, business loans, and consumer loans including credit cards, student loans, and every loan imaginable. He stated this was critical because the entity that had the power to grant the loan had the power to forgive the loan. The assistant director further stated that no loan should be granted to a private business of any kind because that private business would use those funds for the purpose of innovation. Innovation would, as it always had, eliminate jobs for the workers. He further stated that the granting of credit was the best and most efficient way to transfer wealth when credit was granted properly. Properly, he stated, meant that credit would be granted on the request of the borrower, with no requirement to collateralize the loan and no requirement to prove a means of repayment or a willingness to repay. After all, the grantor granted credit with no expectation of repayment.

When the assistant director's appointment became effective, he published a communiqué, stating it was his directive to bring about and enforce, to the letter, all the policies he had put forth in his articles and addresses. The director added her blessing and support and stated this was the policy of the Agency. When asked at the press conference if this was not really enforcing the directive of Karl Marx, the director retorted it was nothing more than re-establishing the directives of the founders of our country by bringing about an equal society, both economically and socially. After all, she went on to state, that it is says in the Declaration of Independence that all men are created equal.

The headlines in the papers the next day stated the Agency, under the new director, wanted to enforce equality to all Americans as promised in the Declaration of Independence. The Marxist/Progressives in Congress hailed this as a new day in America, and the head of the Regime said a great American had been appointed to the directorship of the Agency, as had other great Americans been appointed to other key regulating agencies which had been established to protect the 99% from the 1%.

This was what was happening in the industry and in the country, as their two-year commitment of employment was coming to an end. They would be leaving the corporation in very competent hands. The programmers continued to frustrate the agents and the Agency. Much of their work could now be done off premises, but they were not yet prohibited from going into the institutions, which were not yet considered the property of the people or the government.

The staff he had brought onboard was very competent, but, more importantly they were all committed to preserving a free and independent America. The staff of the corporation understood that private property of individual citizens, including productive property, was vitally important to a free society. It was one of the key elements that set a free society apart from a totalitarian state.

On their last official day of employment, the corporation held a thank you dinner for them. All the employees, Board members, and most of the institution owners, attended. It was a sad and yet, joyous occasion. There were stories told that brought laughter and tears. The pervasive emotion was one of extreme gratitude to both of them. It was obvious their sincerity and dedication to the industry and, most importantly, to a Free America had been greatly appreciated. Even though they would continue to have a role to play in the corporation as consultants, it would not be the same. They appreciated the true friendships they had formed. As a show of gratitude, the Board decided to dispense with the normal plaques, and, instead, gave them a first-class vacation of their choice for their family to be taken within fifteen days. The board told them there would be no consulting demands for the next thirty days and they should enjoy their well-deserved time for fun and relaxation.

CHAPTER 7

It took them a couple of days to relax and slowdown from their hectic pace over the last several years. But warm sun, the cool ocean breezes, white sand, the lazy days, and having the children around, was the best therapy any doctor could have prescribed. They were more grateful to the Board with each passing day. Being away from phones, computers, and newscasts allowed them to refocus on each other and their family. Whether they purposefully avoided the topic, or whether it was through some silent understanding, they never broached the topic of what they would do for work when they returned home.

They did have many discussions, however, about the family and the children's education now that they would begin their schooling. They also had many philosophical and current topical discussions, as well. One afternoon, as they were relaxed on the beach and the children were nearby building sand castles, she told him she wanted to discuss the children's education. She believed they would have to make a decision on whether or not they would have their children attend a public school, a private school, or if they would homeschool.

They lived in an area that, according to all accounts, had one of the finest school systems around. The buildings were relatively new and had been well maintained. The playgrounds had all the proper equipment. She had talked about the schools with mothers in their neighborhood, who had children that attended the schools. These mothers had nothing but good things to say about the teachers and the principal. The PTA seemed to be one of the more active. The PTA had raised substantial funds through fundraisers. A couple of the mothers had served as room mothers and said discipline and order were maintained. The mothers would also talk about how advanced their children's reading skills were.

He knew his wife very well and just kept silent, but attentive, while she was explaining the situation. He knew she was leading to something. Then she started to talk about some of the older children. She said that while visiting with some of the mothers who had older children, she had asked to look at some of their textbooks and was surprised by what she saw. The textbooks talked about the evils of business owners and how these owners were selfish and greedy. She saw one of the textbooks explaining how people like Andrew Carnegie, John D. Rockefeller, Henry Ford, J.P. Morgan, and other American entrepreneurs were evil and greedy. The textbooks went on to explain that these people were able to accumulate great wealth because they exploited the hard-working people of America.

She said she had seen in history textbooks that America became a wealthy and powerful country because it stole all its land and natural resources, from less powerful people, namely, the American Indians and the Mexican Indians. The textbook went on to explain that all-powerful nations had gained their power the same way the American entrepreneur did, and that was through the exploitation of others. The textbooks would go on to conclude that the world would only be fair and just when there was social justice and economic equality between individuals and between nations.

She went on to explain that she had taken it upon herself to do a little research, and she had learned that the teachers' unions had become all powerful. She learned that the teachers' unions were fronts for the Marxist doctrine. Both of them knew how Lenin had insisted on controlling the educational system when the Bolsheviks took power and, like any leader of an ideology, turned the system into an indoctrination system, and not a system of education. In her further research, she had found the leaders of the teachers' unions had made statements about how it was their duty to teach social justice and expose the evils of capitalism. These self-proclaimed Marxists, in many instances, had stated they must teach the Marxist doctrine in the public schools. This, she concluded, was being done, and she did not want to send their children to a center of indoctrination as opposed to a center of education. She believed their only options were to find a private school of which they approved, or they would homeschool the children.

Neither of them knew anybody who had homeschooled their children so they did not have any direct reference. Both had read articles about the advantages and disadvantages. The state was against homeschooling and was not allowing the homeschooled children to participate in any school-sponsored activities of any kind. Even the independent athletic teams, which allowed homeschooled children to participate, were barred from using public school grounds for practice or for actual games. This was due to the direct efforts of the teacher unions. They knew other parents who had homeschooled had found athletic teams on which their children could participate, as well as other social activities for the children.

They thought the two major advantages of homeschooling would be that they would know what their children were being taught and how they were progressing, along with the flexibility they would have. If they wanted to go and spend some time in Europe for instance, the children could go along, and their regular education could continue, along with an advanced education in culture, history, and language. They decided they would not make a decision until they had looked at some of the private schools in the area, but they were leaning heavily toward homeschooling.

The discussion on the beach about homeschooling opened the door to political and philosophical discussions, as well. They, of course, usually avoided these discussions during the day while the children were demanding their attention, as children will do, but took full advantage of the beautiful evenings, the lovely deck, and some wonderful wine to discuss many of the topics they enjoyed, but did not have the time for in-depth discussions over the last couple of years. These discussions centered on their common interest of history, and that led to discussions on the teachings of Karl Marx.

One evening he recalled an incident that had happened several years ago. A well-known pundit on a very popular cable network was doing his typical pontificating. The pundit was explaining how a well-known currency manipulator, who was also a huge contributor to the Marxist/Progressives, could not be a Marxist. The pundit went on to explain that the currency manipulator had made all his money in the capitalists' world and, therefore, could not be a Marxist. After she was done convulsing in laughter, she commented on the huge amount of damage so many of those pompous pundits did. She knew people couldn't make money in a true Marxist society. She was also well aware of the fact that Friedrich Engels made his money in the capitalists' world. Engels was a true believer of the Marxist doctrine. Not only was Engels a huge financial contributor to Marx, and perhaps, the only real friend Marx ever had, but Engels was also a contributor to many of the works of Marx including "The Communist Manifesto." It was also Engels who completed, from the notes of Marx, the second and third volumes of "Das Capital."

The discussion ended with them concurring on how little the American public really knew about the doctrine of Karl Marx. Much of the lack of knowledge was the fault of the American public because they did not take the time, nor did they have the interest to learn about this evil. The educational system would also have to accept a large part of the blame. They knew the educational system had purposefully been turned into an indoctrination system, and a part of that indoctrination was to mislead the public on what Marxism really was and its true evil. This misleading, by the world of academia, had come along with the Marists intentional misleading when teaching history, including American history, and their deliberate rewriting of history to advance their agenda. What was not being taught, for instance, was the fact that Marx, understanding the importance of indoctrination at an early age, had called for public education for all. Marx did this in the middle of the nineteenth century. Now the Marxist/Progressives were calling for public education, literally from the cradle through high school and beyond. Of course, they said it was the responsibility of the government and a right of the parents to have child care for their children from birth. It was not being taught that Lenin said he had three main goals at the time he was consolidating his power in Russia, to become the Soviet Union. Lenin said that he had to control the financial industry, education, and the health care industry. He went on to say that control of the health care industry was really the arch of Marxism.

The next evening they were talking about finding health coverage, now that they were no longer employees of the corporation. This was something they would have to do quickly. They agreed they would talk with an agent as soon as they returned home. They discussed some of the provisions they would need that were particular to them. They said how happy they were that they were still able to make their own choices for their health coverage and care. They wanted to be sure their doctor and the hospital, nearby, would accept the insurance of the insurer they chose.

It was well known that the Marxist/Progressives were promoting universal health care. This was not a recent thought of the Marxist/Progressives. They had been pushing for government control of health coverage and healthcare since at least the middle of the twentieth century. A true American statesman, a conservative, a truly fine man, and an actor who rose to the presidency, stated even prior to the passage of Medicare that the Marxist/Progressives will lie and cheat until they have total control over the health industry of the American public. They both knew it was not the goal of the Marxist/Progressives to provide better health coverage or better healthcare, but it was one of the easiest ways for the government to gain control of 20% of the American economy.

The last true American statesman had warned the American public that the Marxist/Progressives would use every scheme they can. He said they will use the natural sympathies for grandma and grandpa, claiming you are uncaring if you do not want the government to provide for them, even though they were well provided for at the time. Lenin had said, while implementing Marxism and knowing he was lying, that the Russian people would have better coverage and less expensive coverage when it was provided for by the government. They speculated the rest of the evening on the horror the American public would face if somehow a law were passed that would socialize the American health industry. They both agreed, if it happened, it would be short-lived because such a law would be clearly unconstitutional, and the Supreme Court could never rationalize a way to uphold it.

Their final evening on the deck proved to be very prophetic. The children had gone to sleep especially early that evening. The accumulation of sun, sand, ocean, and activity had taken its toll. They began their discussion outlining their immediate priorities when they returned home. Of course, they would have to check with the corporation. They had given it very little thought while they were away. Even though they were no longer employees, they had a responsibility as paid consultants. He would then start to secure health coverage and she would investigate the private schools in the area, and also look into different homeschooling kits, which she was sure would be available.

They reminisced about their journey together, so far, and remembered the first day they met at the pool. He told her how he thought she might be a plant for the Agency, but had hoped it was not true. She admitted she had questions about him, as well. She was wondering why he would be at the pool on a weekday, and why he was so evasive. She said her woman's intuition told her he was all right and not engaged in some sort of illegal activity. She had thought for only a moment to call the restaurant and leave a message for him that she would not be able to meet him. He told her he had hoped against hope that she would not put together a resume and look for a position, especially after he had spoken to his mother-like figure at the Agency. She admitted to something that she had sworn to secrecy, but thought it would be okay to reveal now. His mother- like figure at the Agency had called her after the breakfast, and they had a woman- to-woman talk, the total contents of which she could not, and would not, disclose.

They then began to speculate on the future. What would the country and the world be like in the next five to ten years? What would the country and the world be like when their children had families and what would the country and the world be like for their grandchildren? They were fearful of what the country would become if the country continued down its current path of indifference as to how it was being changed. Their children and grandchildren would not live in the freedom they had known. Already much of that freedom had been taken. The country had been moving toward the Marxist doctrine for a long time. Businessmen were being condemned for building businesses and earning profits. These businessmen were being told they had a duty and an obligation to share their wealth. These businessmen were being told the government should have the right to limit their incomes. These businessmen were being told this was so because they did not build their businesses; the businesses were built through a communal effort of all, so the businessmen must share with all.

Much of America now believed all people were owed an income from the government. The idea of Marx that all income should be centralized in the government was becoming entrenched in the psyche of the people. The government then distributes the income based on the needs of the individual, and not the effort and production of the individual. Marxists/Progressive leaders in the Congress had stated that Americans should be given a guaranteed income, so they could pursue whatever endeavor would make them happy. This was directly from Marx.

The idea that there is no right or wrong, but all people should be able to do whatever makes them happy, was already well entrenched. It was okay to deceive and cheat, so long as you apologized. The long established morals that had determined behavior for centuries were no longer honored or accepted. Marx had said that all long-held principles, religion, and morality must be abolished, and that was happening.

Marx had also stated that in order to bring about his society that would be a totally free and classless society; it would initially take despotic means. It would be necessary, Marx implied, to have a totalitarian state for a while until absolute freedom could, and would, be established. They talked about how the real power and authority in the American system was now centered in the executive branch. The legislative and judicial branches were no longer co-equal and had lost and abdicated many of their checks and balances.

It was getting late and they were tired. They had to catch an early flight home and would have to be up early the next morning. Before they went to sleep that evening, they promised each other they would do everything they could possibly do to make America aware of the destructive direction in which the Marxist/Progressives were taking America. They also promised each other they would never be concerned about being politically correct, but would expose Marxism and the Marxist/Progressives for what it was - a philosophy that could not and never has worked, because it rewards for non-production and punishes those who strive for achievement and excellence. It also is brought about through a totalitarian state, and once a tyrant has power, he will never relinquish that power. All the wonderful promises the tyrant made are revealed too late as blatant lies and total deception. These promises were lies and were only a means of consolidating power.

It was a couple of weeks after they arrived home that they were able to sit down and have a meaningful discussion about their future. They learned the corporation would not be very demanding. They had hired very good people and had trained them well. This would certainly pay off for them so far as time was concerned, and for the benefit of the corporation and the benefit of the institutions. He had a long discussion with the owners of the institutions in Jacksonville and San Diego. They had both expressed their gratitude, again, and explained how pleased they were with the staff.

He had also been able to go over the insurance options with an agent, and he and she had just completed the application designing a health care plan, which fit their needs, and had their doctor and hospital in the network. She had gone over the schooling choices with him, and they both agreed that it was best for the children if they homeschooled. That decision had informally been reached while they were gone, but had now been researched and secured.

The decision that still had to be made was what they would do. They decided they would have a special dinner at home on a weekday evening. They still honored their date night on Fridays and still reserved that time as "us" time. It had served their marriage very well.

They agreed that perhaps the best way to progress would be for each of them to list different things they could do. Of course, both had been thinking about this, off and on, and they had thrown ideas back and forth to each other. One of the ideas, which had been discussed, was for him to become a history professor at the local college. He would have to go back to school and obtain at least a master's degree. She could do the same and teach history or programming. Both admitted they really had no interest in going back to school or doing, what seemed to them, to be a very repetitious job. They also agreed that they really enjoyed working, together. They had worked, together, toward the same goal, relying on each other, but also doing independent work. This was very appealing.

She remembered the idea she had some time ago about him writing a book. She wondered why they could not write a book together. They had different skills and could work, independently, using their individual skills, but bring the total project together. Their ideas and principles were certainly compatible, and it could be fun. If they wrote a book, however, they must decide on a topic, a style, and a targeted reader.

They both remembered their conversation and their commitment that last night at the resort. They had both read all the works of Marx- well not all of 'Das Capital'- they had skimmed through the mundane parts. They had also read many supporting books and writings and understood the Marx philosophy. Books they had read included several biographies of Marx. They knew they would be able to write a very revealing book. Once the decision had been made to write the book, they would have to decide on a style and a targeted reader. They agreed the best way to proceed would be for each to note their thoughts and draft a preliminary outline. That would be a good start, and they could continue from there. That night neither slept very soundly, for ideas were running through their minds. They both awoke excited, anxious to get on with their next challenge together.

CHAPTER 8

The process they chose to write the book proved to be enjoyable for both of them. They had also decided on their targeted reader. The target would be the American who was concerned about the direction the country was being taken. The targeted reader knew it had something to do with the "isms," but did not really understand the "ism" called Marxism, and its destructive nature. This made their endeavor more difficult because they would have to take the convoluted ideas and writings of Marx and present them in modern American English, so the concepts would be understandable. In addition, they wanted to write a book of moderate length so as not to frighten the typical American, who learned and thought in sound bites. They had settled on a final outline that would give the reader a good idea as to who Marx was as an individual, and then develop his primary philosophy of community owned and controlled productive property by eliminating the capitalist, or as Marx had said, to abolish the individuality, independence, and freedom of the capitalist, and to build a totally conforming and totally egalitarian, or as he called it, a classless society.

They had set a challenge for themselves, but they had set and met challenges in the past.

They learned that establishing the target reader and the goal of the book had been the difficult part. The actual research and writing was the fun part. They knew, after a short time, the difficult part of the writing would be to control the size of the book. There was so much to develop and so many different aspects of Marxism they would like to develop, but they had to remind themselves continuously what the real purpose was.

While they were in the writing process, so many events were taking place that gave their project even more meaning and urgency. There was the constant barrage of words and actions against the capitalist, as the Agency continued its effort to control all aspects of the financial industry. There was the continual assault on the education system to have it become even more a propaganda and indoctrination tool of the Marxist/Progressives. Then there was the continual assault on the health industry to completely nationalize it. It was as if Lenin had been reincarnated and was leading this assault on capitalism and freedom in the United States of America.

In addition, the Marxist/Progressives were assaulting the United States Constitution and the Bill of Rights. Both Woodrow Wilson and Franklin Roosevelt had voiced their disdain for the Constitution. They both ignored it and abused it during their reigns. Both Wilson and Roosevelt understood how difficult it was to bring about their desire to change America into an elected dictatorship, by dismissing or negating the legislative and judicial branches of government. Recently one of the more powerful Marxist/Progressives had stated that the American Constitution was a flawed document because it did not mandate or allow for wealth redistribution. That same Marxist/Progressive politician had told a plumber it was the responsibility of a patriotic citizen to share his wealth, once his company had become successful. After all, the Marxist/Progressive stated, it was not the individual that built the business, but all businesses are built through the communal efforts of the community. This concept came directly from the writings of Marx. It was documented that this particular politician had been schooled in the doctrine of Marxism since he was a young child. He learned his lessons well, and his instructors would have been proud, had they seen what a dedicated Marxist he had become.

The Marxist/Progressives were also directly attacking freedoms guaranteed to Americans in the first amendment to the Constitution; speech, press, and religion. Marxist/Progressive members of the Senate and the House had written letters to the IRS telling the IRS they must stop the free speech of groups who were opposing the Marxist/Progressive doctrine. The IRS leadership took this as a direct challenge and directed IRS agents to delay rulings on the tax-exempt status of those organizations by means of harassment and intimidation. When this attempt to prohibit free political speech was made public, members of the Marxist/Progressives feigned outrage and called for a full investigation. As the investigation took place, the IRS officials who were brought before investigating committees, delayed and obstructed the investigations. These IRS officials mislead the committees by telling half-truths and outright lies, which according to the law, is a felony. The Marxist/Progressives who had claimed outrage, initially, now called the investigation a political witch hunt and unworthy of more time or money. Even though documentation proved the

IRS officials had lied, The Department of Justice, who was headed by a faithful Marxist/Progressive, refused to take any action. The Marxist/Progressives knew how important the elimination of free and open political speech was to their ultimate goal of bringing about a totalitarian state, so they could impose the classless society outlined by Marx.

One of the Marxist/Progressives, a member of the House, orchestrated a full onslaught of the federal government against a law-abiding citizen of the United States. What this citizen had done was to start an organization whose purpose was to educate people who would become poll workers on Election Day. This was not a partisan effort, but the stated goal was to teach people the law so that the elections would be conducted in a fair and impartial manner. The Marxist/Progressive house member had been elected in an election where the opposition had challenged the outcome. It was found that people who had died, but had not been purged from the voting role, somehow found a ride from the cemetery to the voting booth (and then hopefully back to the cemetery) where they voted. Many times these deceased people brought their pets to vote, as well. Those who did not have to come from the cemetery, but were proven to be alive, were found to have voted several times. This type of activity was becoming prevalent in elections. When the American citizen showed with compelling evidence that the Marxist/Progressive House member had orchestrated a federal onslaught by having six different federal enforcement agencies investigate this citizen, the House member expressed total indignation and pounded his chest, extolling his dedication to the protection of the individual citizen. To the impartial observer, it was evident the House member had done everything the citizen claimed, but in the newscasts and newspapers, the story was seldom covered, and when it was covered, it was reported the citizen was a hysterical individual.

The Marxist/Progressives had also orchestrated a direct assault against freedom of the press. The founding fathers, which had written the constitution, knew and understood how critical a free press was to a free and open society. These founders understood the press would have faults, and many untruths and half-truths would be printed. Many of the founding fathers had been the subject of these types of attacks. Nevertheless, the founding fathers knew the government could not have control over who was a member of the press, or over what stories the press wrote and printed. The Marxist/Progressives, on the other hand, knew how critical it was for them to control the press. They understood that the majority of the members of the press sympathized with their cause. However, stories the Marxist/Progressives did not want made known to the public were published on other outlets like the Internet, some cable newscasts, and some independent newspapers. In order to combat this, the Marxist/Progressives had bureaucrats placed in the newsrooms of news outlets. These bureaucrats had the power to control, which stories would be, and which stories would not be, published. The public was told this was to protect them from being exposed to frivolous and untrue stories.

One of the Marxist/Progressives in the Senate expanded the attack on the first amendment protected right of a free press, and introduced a bill that would define a journalist. He said this was to protect the honest journalist. Some of the other members of the Senate saw through this thinly veiled attempt at press control and killed the bill. The executive branch understood how critical this control of the press was, and wrote an Executive Order to accomplish the same. Within days of the signing of the Executive Order, another Executive Order was signed that said all journalists would have to be licensed. In order to qualify for a license, the journalist would have to have a college degree in journalism that was earned at a qualifying school. The list of qualifying schools would be published.

During this same time period, the Marxist/Progressives had also instituted, for all practical purposes, a state religion. The freedom of religion clause in the Constitution had come to take on a completely different meaning from what the founders had intended, when they wrote it into the first amendment. These founders had lived under the rule of England, who had as their state church or religion, the Anglican Church. Many of the colonists had come to America for the specific purpose of not having the state, through a state church, dictate how the citizen was to worship. The Marxist/Progressive had taken this concept of freedom of religion and twisted it to accomplish the dictate of Marx when he said it was critical that all religion and morality be abolished. The concept of the Judeo/Christian teachings that had been such an important part of the founding of the United States, and the writing of the Constitution, did not conform to the philosophy of Marx and, thus, the Marxist/Progressives. Recently, Jews and Christians had been persecuted by being charged with crimes for violating laws that were in direct conflict with their beliefs. Some had been jailed and methods of torture that were banned from use against combatant enemies of the United States were approved to be used against these citizens, in order to extract confessions of guilt.

This practice of using the arm of justice against citizens of the United States was not reserved just for the right wing extremists, as defined by the Department of Homeland Security, but it was also extended to those citizens who publically disagreed with the Marxist/Progressive agenda. A law professor had stated that every citizen in the United States commits three felonies of some kind every day. The point the law professor was making was that the Department of Justice could find a way to prosecute any citizen they chose to prosecute at any time they desired. This was happening more and more. As the persecution became more and more bitter, it was being learned that more and more of these persecuted citizens were committing suicide. The method of suicide was always the same. The persecuted citizen would be found dead, in an isolated location, with a single gunshot to the head. The type of pistol that was used was always the same. The local officials would state they were going to do a thorough investigation. However, after a visit by the FBI, the local officials would state their thorough investigation had been concluded and the initial assessment that the persecuted citizen committed suicide by shooting himself in the head was indeed accurate.

This was the political climate in the country when they completed their book. They decided it would be best to self-publish. They made a strategic decision, because of the atmosphere in the country, and listed only him as the author. They also determined that any public acknowledgment, be it complimentary or derogatory, would be his. He insisted this be done as a way to protect her and also the children. They had determined they would also have a website where they would sell the book, write articles, and write commentary. This would also be under his name, although she would play the major role and be the writer. They both commented on how ironic that was. Just like Engels had written many of the articles with Marx's name on them, she was doing the writing and putting his name on the articles.

What an exciting, but also scary, day it was when they received their first shipment of books. They had positive responses from readers and believed they had accomplished the goals they had established. But now the testing was done. They were now entering the real world. Would they be able to sell these books and, hopefully, order more?

They had decided the best way to market the book was to get it into the hands of people who would talk about it to the public. The initial reaction seemed to be that everybody liked the book and they said they would do what they could to help promote the book. Nothing seemed to happen. They learned the major outlets would not take the risk of publicizing the book and face the wrath of the Marxist/Progressives, who had accumulated a great deal of power and were merciless when using that power against people who tried to expose the Marxist/Progressives true intent. Ironically, he had sent one of the books to a friend of his who was involved with one of the very groups the IRS had tried to silence. The friend asked him if he would be willing to be the main speaker at one of the group's meetings. After the meeting, he would be more than welcome to sell books to the attendees who wanted buy it.

They had discussed this possibility and saw it as a way to reach more people and spread the truth about Marxism and how destructive it is. Now they realized this could also be an excellent way of marketing the book. The scheduled talk was to be given in three weeks. Again, there was much to do. A talk would have to be crafted, and he would have to learn it so he could deliver it affectively. Just like with the book, the real challenge to drafting the talk was to keep it on point and not go off on tangents. They again had to determine what the goal was, and they decided the goal was the same goal they had when they wrote the book.

They had the talk written within the first week. The last weeks were spent rehearsing and making small subtle changes. It turned out she was an excellent critic and coach. The talk would take place three hours from their home. She made arrangements for the children so she could go with him. Both were nervous as the time drew near for him to speak. Once he was introduced and began, he noticed the crowd was involved and paying close attention. He started to relax and enjoy the experience. Although he had excellent eye contact with the crowd, he did not look at her. He thought he would lose his concentration if he did. When he concluded the talk, the room was completely silent. Then after what seemed like an eternity, one person stood and started to applaud, then another, and within seconds, everybody in the room was standing and giving him a thunderous ovation. Only then did he look at her. She was standing and applauding with the others. The difference was she had a huge smile of relief and pride.

It turned out the book sales were better than they had hoped. She handled the actual sales, and he signed books for the enthused and excited people. Many times, while talking with the people, he did feel guilty and wanted to say that she had played a huge part in the writing of the book and the crafting of the talk, but he knew he could not.

They had decided they would drive home that night, as opposed to staying overnight and driving back the next day. It turned out to be a wise decision. Both were too excited and would not have been able to get to sleep anyway. The drive home went by very quickly. They had so much to discuss. They saw how this approach would be a very good approach for future marketing. Besides that, they had effectively reached many people and even though some did not buy a book for whatever reason, they came by to thank them for the information. While discussing this she, thinking out loud, wondered why a CD and/or a DVD could not be recorded and made available. That could be a very effective way of spreading the truth, as well. She made a mental note to check into how that could be done.

Within the next week, they had received two invitations to speak at other similar gatherings. They put these engagements on the calendar and were excited at what was happening. She received a call about a week later from a group in a city that was maybe four hours away. The caller introduced himself as the program chair for the group. The group would like him to come and speak at their Thursday evening meeting. The program chair then told her he hosted a radio talk show and would like him to be a guest of his on his radio program Tuesday afternoon. As a guest of the radio program, he could talk about his book and the website. The radio host would announce during the broadcast that his guest would be speaking in town that Thursday evening. The radio host would promote the talk on Wednesday and Thursday afternoons. The book and website would be promoted as well. She was excited when he came home a little later. She had already started to do some research on radio programs. She had learned there were many programs around that were happy to have knowledgeable guests on their programs.

He learned radio was fun; he could do it from any phone, although landlines were preferred, and they could reach large numbers of people. The crowd at the meeting on that Thursday night was the largest group the group ever had. It was also an enthusiastic group, and the questions he was asked that evening seemed to be even more insightful than at any of the other gatherings. Many times the people asking the questions would refer to the radio program.

She began to actively pursue radio programs, and in a short time, he was doing radio several times a week. Many of the hosts would reference the articles she had written and published on the website, and the host would use that article as the basis for the discussion.

As he was on more and more radio, he also noticed he was receiving more speaking invitations. They also noticed a constant increase of hits on their website. They could trace from where the hits were coming, and many of them were from the websites of the groups where he had spoken, as well as the websites from the different radio programs on which he had been a guest. On many of the programs, he was being asked to be a guest on a semi-regular basis. The increased activity in one area would increase the activity in the other two. He was kept busy preparing for radio broadcasts and speaking engagements, both of which he enjoyed. He was also receiving very positive feedback. She was kept very busy doing research, reading, and working with him, keeping them informed and increasing their knowledge.

She had put the idea of a DVD and a CD on the backburner. There just never seemed to be enough time, even though he was asked for CD's and DVD's almost every time he gave a talk. This project was put on the front burner when a group less than an hour away had asked if he could come and talk to their group. The leader of this group had come up with a brilliant idea for their particular group. She had arranged with some local people, who filmed events, to come and film a six-part series she had put together. The leader wanted him to be the second part of this six part series. His talk would be filmed. The leader indicated they would be doing a CD and a DVD so they could make them available to the members of her group. She very quickly asked the leader if they would be given a copy of both, and if so, could they reproduce them and market them. The leader's response was an enthusiastic "yes." The leader went on to say she had been following their work and would be pleased to be a part of it, even in this small way.

Having self-published their book, she felt confident they could also put together the CD and DVD. With some research, she learned they could burn both a CD and a DVD and make copies. She also found a supply house where they could easily, quickly, and inexpensively get all the supplies they would need. She was able to put together a cover they could have printed locally. She was convinced they could produce the CD and the DVD once they had their copy. They found the people at the different talks really did like the idea and they became big sellers. The CD and DVD helped increase book sales as well.

They would periodically perform a search on different search engines on him and on their website. They found many of her articles had been posted on different websites. She always wrote at the bottom of her articles "PLEASE SHARE." People were sharing! They also found notices of people using the DVD for a showing at local events. Where she could find an email address or a way of contacting these groups, she would send them a nice personal note, always using his name. They were still very careful about not having her or the children receive any notoriety. She had only gone to his first speech and never attended another. Even though the children said they wanted to go and see what Dad does, they made a decision to never do this.

More and more strange situations were happening in the country. Bureaucrats were becoming more and more dismissive of Congress. When these bureaucrats were called before Congress to testify, they were arrogant and condescending to the representatives of the people. These bureaucrats told blatant lies and knowingly deceived. This was to be expected, since the person who now held the same office George Washington, Calvin Coolidge, and Ronald Reagan had held, knowingly lied time after time to the American people. The vast majority of the American people said, when polled, that this person could not be believed about any substantive matter. The people said this person would lie to bring about his agenda, which was now understood to be by over 60% of the knowledgeable public, the same agenda put forth by Karl Marx.

Different bureaucratic agencies were accumulating vast amounts of weapons and ammunition. When questioned, these agencies would deny this activity. Citizens were having their communications traced by the government. There were rumors that the government was hacking into computers of individuals and businesses without even seeking a search warrant. She had noticed some strange happenings on her computer. One day while she was writing an article, she saw her face in place of the document. It was only for a split second, so she dismissed it as her imagination. She did, however, put tape across all the cameras on the computers.

There had also been more and more strange suicides by people who had openly talked against the agenda of the current occupant of the White House. The Department of Justice dismissed these as disgruntled people who had obviously realized they were wrong in their thinking, and once they understood the truth, these people were so embarrassed they decided to take the easy way out of their situation. The country was very polarized, and this was augmented by that same White House occupant who would demonize and denigrate his opponents, and then chastise those opponents for not being willing to work with him. It was obvious that cooperation was not what he wanted. The polarization and antagonism was very good for his cause of fundamentally transforming the country into a Marxist society, as he had promised he would do.

CHAPTER 9

They both continued their life long practice of reading books that supported the Marxist philosophy, and they also watched programs and debates of Marxists supporters. Her military father had taught her this. He said the great military minds throughout history were great because they understood their enemies better than the enemy understood them. Her father said that was why he admired such great military men as Alexander the Great, Julius Caesar, Napoleon Bonaparte, and Robert E Lee. He, on the hand, had been taught this same concept out of necessity and the school of hard knocks.

One evening when the children were in bed and the computers were off, they found themselves watching a debate on cable television that was sponsored by the Marxist/Progressive Think Tank Center for American Progressiveness. The founder of the Think Tank was on the panel, along with a Marxist/Progressive Senator from New York and a Marxist/Progressive House Member from Minnesota. They found the irrational arguments and the dream of a fictitious utopia entertaining and educational for them. They could always hear the direct quotes and ideas from Marx in these discussions.

This particular discussion went in a different direction and became personal to them. The founder of the Think Tank started to express outrage about the right wing extremists in the United States who were spreading falsehoods and lies about the Marxist/Progressive movement. He went on to say these extremists were more dangerous to the United States than any foreign terrorist, and they must be stopped and eliminated. He said it was the constitutional duty of the Department of Justice to capture these terrorists and treat them as any enemy combatant would be treated. These extremists did not deserve and should not receive any of the constitutional protections, because they were not loyal and conforming citizens the founder claimed.

When the Senator and House Member chimed into the discussion, they argued, that Congress had a duty to hold hearings and expose this danger for all to see. The founder of the Think Tank said he would not only oppose such hearings, but would prevent them from taking place. He said this exposure would just give these terrorists more of a platform to spread their lies and hate. The Think Tank founder went on to say that the Department of Homeland Security should quietly and meticulously capture these terrorists. When they are captured, the founder went on to say, it should be done in such a way as to eliminate the terrorist while not leaving any trace of a capture, so as to not raise suspicions that the government was ever involved. The founder said that even though the government had the duty and the right to carry out such actions, because of the direct threat to the security of the country by these less-than-human individuals, it could damage the movement of the Marxist/Progressives to bring about a free and classless society with absolute freedom.

She and he sat in total silence and disbelief as this discussion was happening on a publicly broadcasted television station. They were astounded that no comment of further disagreement was uttered by either the Senator or the House Member. Nobody in the audience asked about, or questioned in any way, what the founder had said, during the question and answer period. Two of the questions alluded to the comment, not to oppose, but to totally support the founder and his conclusion.

After they turned off the television, they had a very subdued discussion. They discussed the fact that anybody would say such outrageous things on public television. It did not surprise them that people in the Marxist/Progressive movement believed and supported this position, but that they had become that brazen. They talked about how the Constitution had been so badly twisted as to be used as a tool to bring about the totalitarian state called for by the Marxist/Progressives. They talked about how the American public had been so indoctrinated, through the school system and the press that many would believe the actions called for by the founder were indeed, legal under the Constitution.

She was very quiet in her outrage and became quieter and quieter as the discussion continued, until the discussion had become a monologue by him. When he realized he was doing all the talking, he stopped talking and looked at her. She had tears running down her cheeks. She moved close to him and put her head on his shoulder and began to sob. He just held her and let her cry through the pain, thinking it was for the country she was crying. When she had regained control, she looked at him and told him that, yes, she was sad because of what the country her father had served, and she loved, was becoming, but the tears were because the very person the founder had called a terrorist was him, and she feared for his life.

The next day they saw only two stories on the discussion from the prior night. Both stories were short, with only one briefly questioning if the intent of the constitution was to eliminate constitutional rights for any American citizen who had been classified as a terrorist. The reporter believed they still had a right to a trial, but in such a situation, the burden of proof should be shifted to the defendant as opposed to the state. They learned a couple of days later, that the cable station which usually reported openly on such issues, had been warned by the FCC that their license would be pulled if they accurately reported on the discussion. The General Manager chose not to allow the story to be reported at all.

He incorporated the story into his talk and into his radio interviews. She wrote about it in her blog and then wrote an article that was re-published on many other blogs. Only a few other people, who had become known as the opposition, had seen the discussion. Within twenty-four hours of the discussion, no trace of it could be found. It had been wiped clean, and when the founder was asked about it, he denied he had made any such statements and those who were reporting his statements had taken him totally out of context. The founder said he had stated that many Americans opposed to the new freedom, had openly called for terrorist activities against the government. In spite of their calling for acts of terrorism, they were still citizens and that was the beauty of our constitution; it still protected them. When the founder was asked why the discussion could not be seen, he simply answered he had been told it was because of a computer crash.

She noticed more and more irregularities on their website. Articles she had posted were somehow missing. She would re-post them, and a short time later they would be missing, again. She went on her computer one morning, only to find it was turned on already. Looking at her history, it said the last website opened was hers. She had been doing some research and personal work the night before, and she knew she had not looked at her website as her last computer task.

He had noticed different people in his audiences that he had never noticed before. These were people who appeared not to know anyone else. They did not engage in conversation with anybody and when approached, would say hello and quickly make an excuse to leave. He also noticed these people would take notes. That was not, by itself, unusual however, but their note taking was done not while he was speaking, but mostly prior to his speaking and then seemed to be based on his actions and not his words.

As the Marxists/Progressives accumulated more and more power, and the people became less and less free, he was in greater and greater demand for speaking engagements and for radio interviews. The hits on the website grew by leaps and bounds and her articles were being reprinted with increasing frequency. The pace had grown every bit as hectic as it was in those first eighteen months when they became employees of the corporation. She determined they both needed a break from the pace, and the children needed some time with them. She decided they should take some time where the children would be their focus and they would have some time to focus on each other, again.

She decided to make arrangements for them to go to a small, isolated island in the South Pacific. He needed to have his passport renewed, and so, she took it to the passport office with all the required material. The passport agent explained to her that if she was willing to pay an extra fee, they could have the renewal expedited, and there should be no problem having it in time for them to take their vacation.   She agreed that would be a good idea. The agent looked at his computer and then asked to be excused because there seemed to be a slight problem. Through the open window, she could see the agent talking to his supervisor. After the supervisor checked his computer she could see him making a phone call. The supervisor was on the phone for a few minutes and then both the agent and the supervisor came out to meet with her. The supervisor explained there would be a delay in issuing the passport; in fact, he was not sure if they could issue it. The supervisor said he was not given a reason, but he had seen this happen a few times in the past year. The supervisor told her he was sure it was just some misunderstanding. In any case, it would take at least six months to issue the passport, and in the meantime the supervisor said they would have to keep the old passport.

She left the office a very frightened wife. She began to question their decisions to move forward with the book, speaking, website, and other activities. As she reflected on their decision-making process, she recalled the evening they had decided they would do something that mattered. She recalled the process they went through when they chose a topic for their book, she remembered the pride she had the evening of the first talk, not just of him, but what they had done together, and she recalled how they had decided that these activities were very important. She just did not realize that in the country she loved, the government would become the ruler and the citizens the servants. This was in complete contrast to what the founders established, how they wrote the Constitution, and their intent. The founders had warned the public that it would take a diligent citizenry if freedom was to be maintained, because there were many people who believed society was better for all if all aspects of society were controlled by them. She understood the price they might have to pay would be high, but the cause was just.

Now that they were unable to go out of the country, she would have to make alternative plans. She remembered the owner of the San Diego institution had a quiet and isolated beach house north of San Diego. She would call him and see if they might rent the beach house for ten days or so. The San Diego owner was delighted to hear from her and had many questions. All the institution owners were readers of their blog and had kept abreast of what was happening. The owner explained the consensus of the industry was that her husband might be a target and he should be extremely careful. She told the owner about the discussion they had heard on television and some of the strange situations they had encountered, including the one at the passport office, and that was the purpose for her call. She then went on to explain how they needed some down time and she was wondering if they could rent his beach house. The owner told her absolutely not, but they could use it for as long as they wished. He had only one condition, and that was that they would set aside one evening for a barbecue with the San Diego owner and his wife.

She cleared the schedule and they were on their way. Everybody was excited. They arrived late in the afternoon and did not want to go out to dinner, so went to the nearby grocery store and did a full scale-shopping run. The children were old enough to be a part of the meal preparation.

They prepared dinner as a family that evening and it help everybody to immediately relax. The next several days were peaceful and relaxing; no rushing anywhere and no schedules to keep. They all tried surfing and were surprisingly good. They had their volleyball game every day. The teams of she and their son and he and their daughter were the most competitive. They especially enjoyed the late afternoon and early evening beach walks and family talks. The children were very well versed in the work of their parents and very well read. The decision to homeschool had been a very good one. Even with the homeschooling, the children were socially well adjusted and adults had always commented on the maturity of the children.

The day arrived when the owner of the San Diego institution would be coming over for the barbecue. The owner had called, earlier, and said for them not to worry about a thing; he would bring everything for dinner, including wine. The only thing the owner asked them to do was to be ready for a nice evening. They were outside enjoying the beach weather when they noticed not one, but several cars coming up the road. They recognized the San Diego owner's car, but the other cars all looked like rental cars.

As the cars came closer, they started to recognize the people in the other cars. All the owners who had been on the board when the corporation purchased their business, and their wives, had come to San Diego and the beach house, just to spend the evening with them. This included the Jacksonville owner and his wife.

They had a wonderful and fun evening with so many stories to be told. All commented on their children and what wonderful young adults they had become. Any discussion about the threat, of which all were aware, was avoided. This was an evening for levity, friendship, great food, and great wine. All understood this. The evening passed by quickly, and when it was time for the owners and their wives to leave, the atmosphere quickly changed. The mood became one of finality, as if this was a group of elderly people who knew they would never see this moment and possibly these friends, again. A few tears did appear. The good-byes were never spoken, just silently understood as if all knew the inevitability of the coming days, weeks, months, and years. The owners got into their cars and drove away as the family stood next to each other, not waving, but arm in arm.

The last two days the family had on the beach became a time of reflection and thought. The children had lots of questions about their parents; how they had met, why they did what they did, why they decided to homeschool them, and questions about their childhoods and their parents. It was a time of bonding; parent and child, husband and wife, and brother and sister. They were all very reflective on the drive to the airport and the airplane ride home. All were very glad they had that time together, including the evening with the owners and their wives.

The very next day they were all immediately back in the routine they had escaped. He had radio broadcasts and two talks that week. She had articles to write and updating to do on the website. They had emails they had to answer and phone calls to return. An email had come from a state association asking if he would be the keynote speaker at their annual meeting. The meeting would be held in a resort that was in the mountains and about a two-hour drive from the nearest airport. The email said somebody from the association would be glad to meet him at the airport and take him to the meeting and then back to the airport the next day. They decided this was a marvelous opportunity and accepted the invitation. The meeting would be held in three months, so they had more than adequate time to prepare for the talk. They sent the usual bio and photo for the association to use for promotion. They thanked the association for the offer to meet him at the airport but explained it would be easier if he just rented a car. The association did a full promotion campaign and all anticipated a very large turnout.

The next couple of months were very uneventful for them. The usual assaults of the Marxist/Progressives were taking place every day. More regulations were being passed and more Executive Orders were being signed. The occupant of the White House had continued his assault on the Constitution and the opposition; meanwhile, blaming everybody else for the economic condition of the country and the loss of influence the country had suffered abroad. She did not, however, notice any strange happenings with her computer. He no longer noticed any of those different people at any of his talks. One evening, as they were talking, she commented on how quiet things had been. Maybe they had been taken off the radar, he speculated hopefully.

He was prepared for his talk at the association's annual meeting. As he typically did, he arranged to take an early morning flight so he would not be rushed and he would be able to make adjustments if a flight was late. Arrangements had been made for a rental car. The association had arranged for a room for him that evening, so it was one thing he did not have to do. He left the house for the airport the next morning, before anybody else was awake. This was not unusual. He would call her after he had landed, picked-up the rental, and had driven a few miles out of the city. This was the normal routine. He had also arranged to let the program chair of the association know when he arrived at the resort, which he thought would be early afternoon. This would give him time to check into the room, take a short nap, then shower, and dress for the meeting. He always liked to be early so he could put out books, CD's, and DVD's. Many people would buy what they wanted before his talk, so they would not be in the rush after the talk. This was also a good time to meet and speak personally with the attendees.

The plane arrived early. He was glad that he would have a little extra time. He always carried his luggage onto the airplane so he would not have to wait for luggage but he could go right to the car rental bus that would take him over to the car center. He had been through this airport a number of times and was familiar with the routine. As he left the secured area of the airport, two large men dressed in dark suits and wearing sunglasses fell in step with him; one on either side. They told him the association had arranged for them to meet him and take him to the resort. This, they said, would make it easier for him. He knew this was not true. The association never said anything to him about transportation after he told them it would be easier for all if he just rented a car.

He told the men they had mistaken him for somebody else because he had other transportation plans and began to walk ahead of them. He realized he was their target when the men fell in step with him again. One of the men then made sure he saw a pistol that nobody else could see. The other man told him they knew who he was, and they had orders to provide his transportation. He would accept their offer one way or another.

She knew he should have landed, rented his car, and started to drive to the resort. That meant that she should have heard from him by now, but no phone call. After an hour or so, she checked with the airline to be sure his plane had landed on time. Learning that it did, she checked with the car rental company and she was told that he had rented his car about an hour ago. This seemed strange, but, then, maybe he was in an area where his phone did not have service. He was driving through the mountains. She felt better knowing he had rented the car and thought he would call when he arrived at the resort.

The time had come and gone when he should have reached the resort, and still no call. She called the resort and was told he had not checked into his room. She was able to reach the program chair and the program chair said he had not contacted her, yet. No, the program chair said, the weather was clear and she did not know of any problems coming over the pass. In fact, some people had arrived at the resort just a short time ago, and said it was an easy and pleasant drive all the way. She thanked the program chair and asked if she would call as soon as she had heard from him, maybe he had a problem with his phone.

About an hour before the social hour was to start, she checked with the hotel and the program chair, again. By now he should have arrived. When she was again told he had not checked into his room or checked with the program chair, she became very worried. She recalled very vividly the statements of the founder of the Marxist/Progressive Think Tank on television that evening. She thought of all the supposed suicides, which had been reported over the last couple of years. She thought of all the different people he had described that were at his talks, as well as the strange happenings that had occurred on her computer.

Hoping against hope that her imagination had just been running wild, she called the State Highway Patrol of the state of the association. The Highway Patrol told her they could not comment on any accidents that might have or might not have taken place on any highway in the state, unless they knew whom she was. She told them her name, and the comment was how sorry they were, but they were not able to make any comments without proof by an independent source that she was who she said she was. She had never heard of a policy like that, but knew she would not get an answer, no matter how much she begged. The children were aware of their mother's state of distress and asked what was wrong. She explained that she did not think anything was seriously wrong, but their dad had not arrived for his speaking engagement, yet. She was sure he had a flat tire or something of that kind, and that they would hear from him soon.

Late that evening, she heard a knock on the door. Looking through the peephole, she saw an official looking man standing outside. She asked through the door who it was and what he wanted. The man answered he was from the government, and he had news for her about her husband, would she open the door. She was very frightened for her husband, for her children, and for herself and told the man she felt uncomfortable opening the door. The man said he understood and if she preferred, she should get her phone and he would call her from outside to give her the news; it would be better than shouting through the door. Before she reached her phone, it was ringing. When she answered, the man said he was the person outside. She went back to the door and when she looked through the peephole, she could tell it was him that was talking to her.

The man said he was sorry he had to deliver this news to her, this way, but would respect her wishes. The government man went on to explain that a car had been found on a mountainous highway in the same state her husband had been scheduled to speak. The government man went on to explain that the car was badly burned and the burned body of a man was found inside the car. The body had been burned beyond recognition. The government had been able to tell the burned man had committed suicide because they were able to detect a single gunshot to the head. The government speculated the man shot himself while driving and then the car plunged off the cliff and burst into flames. The government had identified the man as her husband. The burned car was identified as the rental car her husband had rented that morning. In addition, they found his wallet, which had not burned, and it contained his identification. She knew immediately this was a fabricated story about the man being her husband. He never carried or used a wallet. She also knew he would never take his own life and leaves her and the children. She kept those thoughts to herself.

She woke the children and told them what the government man had told her. She told them she knew the man found in the car was not their father. She did not know what had happened to their father, but she was absolutely certain he was not the dead man in the car. She told the children they should not mention this to anyone and they should follow her lead in the next several days. When the state offered her the charred remains of what they claimed were her husband's remains, she refused them without any explanation. She and the children did not hold a memorial service of any kind.

The following morning he was awakened and felt so horrible, he knew he had been drugged. He was in a windowless room. The only furniture in the room was the army cot on which he was laying. A guard was standing by the door. The two men he met at the airport came into the room and told him it was breakfast time and he was to come with them. They took him into another room that had a television. The television was turned to the local news. He heard the reporter talking about a car accident that had happened the day before on a mountain road. The reporter explained that the driver had shot himself in the head while driving and the car had plunged down a cliff. Both car and driver were burned beyond recognition. Authorities were able to identify the driver by the driver's license they found which had not burned. Authorities learned the dead man had been a right wing extremist, a terrorist, and an enemy of the state. The authorities would not reveal his name because his fellow terrorists would make him into a martyr. The two men told him that the man at the bottom of the cliff was him, and his wife and children had already been informed.

For the next period of time, he was not sure how long; he was tortured physically and mentally. He was given only enough food and water to keep him alive. He was constantly asked who else was in his organization and what did his wife know. He told them she knew absolutely nothing. She had no idea what he was doing and she believed he was a motivational speaker. No matter the pain, his story never changed. One of the young men, who stood guard over him, after he had been brought to his room from a torture session, would try to make him as comfortable as possible. He knew this young man had a good heart, and they developed a mutual respect.

One day, after a particularly bad beating at the hands of a person he recognized as the founder of the Marist/Progressive Think Tank, he knew his final breath was very near. He had never seen or heard such hatred as he saw from that founder. When he was taken back to his room and the young man was trying to make him comfortable, he told the young man not to be concerned for him. But he did ask the young man if he would do something for him that was very important to him. The young man agreed. He motioned for the young man to come closer so he could whisper to him. After whispering, he said thank you, turned his head, mumbled something, and took his last breath.

A few weeks later she was walking in the park. She heard the voice of what seemed to be a young man behind her. The young man said she should not turn around but she should just keep walking. The young man said he had a message from her husband. Her husband had asked him to deliver it to her. He had only a minute. If he took longer they both could be in danger. She told him she understood and kept walking. The young man told her he was the guard of her husband and had come to respect him very much. Because of her husband, he had read his book and read articles he had written on the Internet. He now realized her husband was right in everything he had said. Because of that, he was delivering this message to her. The young man said her husband knew, she knew, he had not committed suicide, and that the body found in the car was not his. He did not know whose body it was. He had been kidnapped and taken someplace else. He wanted her to be sure the children knew that, as well. He also wanted her to be sure to tell the children how much he loved them and how proud he was of the people they were becoming. Her husband wanted her to know she was the love of his live. He loved her more than he could ever have imagined and wanted to thank her for all the joy and happiness she had brought him. Her husband also wanted her to know that he wanted her to stay with the children as long as she could, but he would be waiting for her in heaven, with open arms where they would spend eternity together. The young man told her the final words whispered to him in her husband's message to her were, "so good-bye, my love, for now."

 The young man then told her that he wanted her to know, that her husband then turned his head and just before taking his last breath he heard her husband say, "Good-Bye Constitution, Freedom, America."

ABOUT THE AUTHOR

Don Jans are a father and grandfather. He has read and studied history from a very early age. For some reason he found Russian history to be especially interesting. This led him to the study of Karl Marx and Marxism. As he began to understand what Marx taught, he learned it was different from what he had been taught in school. He also learned that Americans do not understand or know what Marxism professes. That discovery led to his writing his first book "My Grandchildren's America." This book is a straight forward, simple introduction to Karl Marx and Marxism.

After writing that book the author was asked to speak at a local function. This led to him speaking across the country. If your group is interested in having him speak to them, contact the author via email. The email address is on his website. It has been written and stated by people who have heard him speak, that he is the best speaker they have ever heard. You can read comments on his website www.mygrandchildrensamerica.com. At this website you can also read many articles he has written. In addition, there are links to different broadcasts where he was the guest.

CPSIA information can be obtained
at www.ICGtesting.com
Printed in the USA
FFOW05n0045080914